PHOTOTRUTH OR PHOTOFICTION?

Ethics and Media Imagery
in the Digital Age

Tom Wheeler
School of Journalism and Communication
University of Oregon

2002

LAWRENCE ERLBAUM ASSOCIATES, PUBLISHERS
Mahwah, New Jersey   London

Acquisitions Editor: Linda Bathgate
Textbook Marketing Manager: Marisol Kozlovski
Editorial Assistant: Karin Bates
Cover Design: Kathryn Houghtaling Lacey
Textbook Production Manager: Paul Smolenski
Full-Service & Composition: UG / GGS Information Services, Inc.
Text and Cover Printer: Hamilton Printing Company

This book was typeset in 11/13 pt. Times Roman, Bold, and Italic. The heads were typeset in
ITC Serif Gothic Bold, ITC Serif Gothic Light, and ITC Serif Gothic Regular.

Lawrence Erlbaum Associates, Inc., Publishers
10 Industrial Avenue
Mahwah, New Jersey 07430

Library of Congress Cataloging-in-Publication Data

Wheeler, Tom
    Phototruth or photofiction? : ethics and media imagery in the digital age / Tom Wheeler.
        p. cm.
    Includes bibliographical references and index.
    ISBN 0-8058-4261-6 (pbk. : alk. paper)
        1. Photojournalism—moral and ethical aspects. 2. Image processing—Digital
techniques—Moral and ethical aspects. 3. Mass media criticism. I. Title.

TR820 .W4 2002
174'.9070—dc21

                                                                                    2002017492

Books published by Lawrence Erlbaum Associates are printed on acid-free paper,
and their bindings are chosen for strength and durability.

Printed in the United States of America

10   9   8   7   6   5   4   3   2   1

For Daniel, Matthew, and Joe, who inspired this book
by often asking the same question while watching television:
"Hey, Dad, is this real?"

Brief Contents

Contents

Foreword

James D. Kelly

It has been 20 years since computers were first used to process photographic imagery in the mass media. Almost since the first day, photojournalists have expressed concern about the computer's ability to alter the realistic imagery captured by their cameras. The ethics of digital imaging have increasingly dominated discussions among journalists—first the photographers, then their editors, and finally their managers.

The chemical photograph with its imperceptible transition from black to white through an infinite number of grays seemed for more than a century so easy to understand. A photo was reality. It was a scientific document. We could understand how lenses worked and could predict how chemical reactions would occur, and we believed the photograph was as objective as mathematics and as clear a view as glass provides.

Now, at the start of the 21st Century, photography has passed from the confident realm of chemistry to the ethereal world of electronics. For more and more people, a photograph is simply a bit of software, a long series of 0's and 1's that are more like an idea than a crystal of salt or the fibers of the paper you now hold in your hand. Indeed, you cannot hold a digital image at all. While a negative is a thing, a JPEG file is more a formula than anything tangible. Each formula is built from essentially the same components—sequences of binary bits. Rearrange the bits a little and you have a spreadsheet of numbers. Rearrange them again and you have a poem by Longfellow.

This most postmodern of phenomena is generally called convergence. It seems that everything can be represented by a formula that a computer can read to generate a semblance of the original. A human voice is rendered as a string of digits and emanates from the silvery surface of a CD. Or the formula could be a picture of the singer's face, or the words she used to compose the song, or the sales figures for that little disk of plastic. The direct relationship between the media that stores the creative work and the work itself is gone now. A negative is not a piece of acetate. A musical score is not paper. A painting is not canvas.

This convergence has transformed all of our symbolic creations—numbers, letters, lines, shapes, notes, songs, whispers, cries, stories, and legends—into strings of simple switches that are either open or closed, on or off, yes or no. What were once beautifully different things are now converted into strangely similar nonthings.

The sequence of binary data that is a digital photograph is the same regardless of the medium on which it is stored: floppy disk, hard drive, CD-ROM, or even numbers printed on a piece of paper; the thing it is stored upon is not representational. The photograph is just a bunch of digital bits, as simple as black and white. Odd then that this ultimate in simplicity, this fundamentally either/or standard, should have set off so much discussion about the gray areas of photojournalism. It is the ultimate paradox of media.

Today the software that changes a frozen moment of time into a moment that never was is available to everyone with a personal computer. Some people are even ready to give up on the truth of photography altogether, as if the truth were resident in a magical place called a darkroom. They claim photography is dead. But the analogy of photographic truth to scientific rendering never fit, and it is quite obviously even more flawed now. Today all the world knows that a photograph is nothing more than a formula for arranging dots into a pattern that looks like something. Rearrange the dots on the computer screen and the pyramids are closer together. Rearrange the dots and a man is pregnant. Rearrange the dots and your ex-spouse never went on that vacation with you to the mountains.

Much to their credit, photojournalists recognized early on that the ease with which a computer could alter a photograph was a threat to their professional credibility, and they began discussing the potential impact. The initial reaction was to more forcibly cling to the known. The National Press Photographers Association defended the reality of the photographic image and pledged never to alter it. The Associated Press said they would not do anything on the computer that could not be done in a darkroom. For two decades photojournalists have engaged in an increasingly sophisticated dissection of what photographs mean to the reading public, of what history reveals about the veracity of photography in the past, and about what photographic reporting is at its very essence. This self-examination has stirred up issues far more fundamental than simply the impact of another new technology. It has unearthed basic questions that are tied more firmly to philosophical notions of truth and meaning than to chemical processes.

The emerging realization is that photojournalism derives its meaning, its value to society, not from chemistry but from credibility. Readers do not believe the photos themselves; they believe the people who make the photos and present them as honest depictions of what happened in the community. Photojournalists are coming to understand something that has always been true: Reality is a mental construct, not a physical state; truth is a human quality, not a property of scientific process.

It has been a comfort for photojournalists to rely on a magical darkroom to justify why their photographs should be believed. It was easy to rest upon these illusions of science. It was fun being the master of the mysterious. But photojournalists are coming to see that they have no magic at all. Instead, they realize that the believability of their visual reports is based upon the exact same bedrock that supports the work of their fellow journalists. We have always known that words can lie. Now everyone knows that photographs can lie, too. Like writers, photographers must now base their claims of reliability on their professional character, on their reputation, on their sacred honor.

Tom Wheeler has provided photojournalists with a perfectly logical way to look at what we do and to gauge the appropriateness of our actions in light of this new realization. This book critically examines the myths, metaphors, and memories of photography and then proposes an analogy between photography and writing that can guide journalists through the next 20 years and beyond. Wheeler's powerful analogy links us to reporters—the people we work most closely with and with whom we share a passion for the truth.

The distinctions between fiction and nonfiction are well known and understood by writers of all persuasions. Journalists write nonfiction. Their readers expect it and count on it. Wheeler provides us with a path to photographic nonfiction—to recognize it, to create it, and to protect it.

The young photojournalists entering the profession today were born after the Scitex machine moved the pyramids on the cover of *National Geographic*. Some barely know the darkroom and therefore cannot live by a code that swears allegiance to its practices. But they do come to photojournalism with a passion for storytelling that is honest and true. Tom Wheeler's analyses, protocols, and tests arm them with tools they can understand in the digital world to which they were born.

James D. Kelly, Ph.D., is an Associate Professor in the School of Journalism at Southern Illinois University Carbondale, and Editor of *Visual Communication Quarterly*.

Introduction

" . . . doomsayers, arguing that the computer is laying waste to any credibility photography has left, declare that the medium is dying. . . . But most of the photographs that are being altered are the ones that were always altered by retouching . . . It's in news and documentary that the unvarnished truth matters. There it's still told, and there we still believe it. The camera continues to work with spunk and vigor on the creation of memories, and no one has stopped looking. The reports of photography's death have been greatly exaggerated."

—*Life*, Spring 1999

There are a hundred reasons not to trust mass-media photography, and yet we do. Or at least we used to. Despite our knowing that cameras can lie, that some photos—even famous ones—were faked in one way or another, for more than a century we have nevertheless bestowed upon photography a remarkable measure of trustworthiness. Now, however, we are inundated with photorealistic yet patently false images. These imposters are so pervasive that authentic photos may soon be looked upon as the exceptions, mere throwbacks to a more naive, pre-cyber era.

The implications are obvious. A weakening of faith in photographic authenticity may undermine the credibility of visual journalism in all its forms: newspapers, magazines, broadcast television, cable, online and so on. While the ramifications are significant, even grave, many working journalists have only recently begun to examine them. Among other goals, this book is intended to help them do so in a thoughtful, practical manner. It neither condemns nor discourages the increasing use of digital technologies (inevitable in any case) but rather suggests guidelines for their responsible application.

If photography's credibility is to endure even within the confines of news media, we must establish more concrete ground rules. In addition, we must look beyond professional and academic discussions to accommodate public attitudes. After all, it is readers and viewers—rather than professors or journalists—who will decide whether photography's credibility survives the increasingly common manipulation afforded by software. So far we have failed to adequately address issues of public perception, such as readers' differing expectations when considering, say, the front page of *The Washington Post* versus the cover of *Spin,* or whether readers draw the distinctions so often cited by professionals when making ethical choices about photos: "hard news" (wars, crime scenes, etc.) versus "soft features," or magazine covers versus interior photos.[1]

Digital photography has been in use for three decades or so, although most early applications entailed military, scientific, law enforcement, or big-budget entertainment pursuits. Professor Fred Ritchin's *In Our Own Image: The Coming Revolution in Photography* (Aperture, 1990; reissued 1999) was the first book to explore the ethics of digital imagery in mainstream media, as well as its effects on attitudes toward the nature of photography itself. Another book, William J. Mitchell's *The Reconfigured Eye: Visual Truth in the Post-Photographic Era* (MIT Press, 1992), explored the cultural and social implications of digitally manipulated visual media. In the years since the publication of those seminal works, photographers, critics, and educators have addressed these topics in articles and at conferences. Notorious manipulated images have sparked still more debate, and many practitioners profess to have learned valuable lessons.

Yet it is difficult to say how far we have come. New image-manipulation devices range from expensive software for media professionals to cheap toys for kids. As these products flood more niches of the consumer market, as we become more accustomed to seeing manipulated images (and more accustomed to manipulating them ourselves), and as questions about ethical responsibility and the lines between illustration and photojournalism continue to defy easy answers, the implications of what everyone calls the digital revolution are beginning to sink in.

Of course, revolutions may be exhilarating, but they are unsettling as well. We have advanced beyond perceiving these miraculous technologies merely as providers of new tools and toys to also contemplating their more sobering effects—upon photographers' control of their work, upon image makers' abilities to deceive, upon public faith in mass-media images of all kinds, even photojournalism.

Regardless of our outlook, we might wonder if we really need a book to explain matters of right and wrong. If we agree that misleading the public is unethical, why discuss it further? How much of a guideline do we require, beyond "If it's wrong, don't do it"? In fact, professionals do not agree on what is right and what is wrong. Digital imagery is here and, ethically speaking, we are not ready for it.

As was the case before the advent of digital media, professionals are especially conflicted about the appropriateness of manipulating images within the vast domain between "hard news" and acknowledged visual fiction. In fact, they disagree as to whether nonfiction photography has much of a future at all. For some, the battle is already lost. Others believe that nonfiction photography will not only survive but may flourish anew as technological innovations unfold, particularly on the World Wide Web.

The point here is neither to resolve nor to rehash old debates about ethics but rather to reexamine them in light of new developments. This book asserts that in the digital age the tenets of good journalism still hold, even if they must be reinterpreted to accommodate evolving technologies and restructured media systems. Rather than telling readers what they must do, it explains long-standing visual-media guidelines, suggests how they might be adapted, and poses questions readers might consider as they make their own decisions.

Specifically, *Phototruth or Photofiction? Ethics and Media Imagery in the Digital Age* has two goals. One is to provide a framework for critical discussion among professionals, educators, students, and concerned consumers of newspapers, magazines, online journals and other nonfiction media. The other is to offer a method of assessing the ethics of mass-media photos (particularly with regard to their processing or alteration)—one that will help visual journalists to embrace new technologies while preserving their own stock in trade: their credibility.

Chapter 1 recounts the invention of photography and how it came to be accorded an extraordinary degree of trust. Chapter 2 details how photos were staged, painted, composited, and otherwise faked (sometimes outrageously) long before the dawn of digital technology. Chapter 3 lists contemporary image-altering products and practices, and speculates that their increasing acceptance will likely influence public perceptions of all mass-media imagery for generations to come. Chapter 4 details many examples of manipulated images in nonfiction media (and the resulting threat to the credibility of the photograph in all its forms), while Chapter 5 lists some of the rationales offered in defense of such manipulations.

Chapter 6 explains how current ethical principles have been derived from the teachings of ancient Greeks and various Enlightenment thinkers, as well as from the Bible, the First Amendment, and other sources. Chapters 7 through 9 continue to lay groundwork for an ethical protocol by explaining long-standing conventions of taking, processing, and publishing journalistic photos. Chapters 10 through 12 outline my concepts of the nonfiction photographic environment (broader than "photojournalism"), a range of implied authenticity, the reader's "Qualified Expectation of Reality," and "photofiction."

Chapters 13 and 14 offer tests for assessing the appropriateness of altered images in nonfiction media, while Chapters 15 and 16 examine the wording and prominence of disclosures of alterations. Chapter 17 examines so-called cosmetic retouching. The final chapters summarize how the book's tests and principles might be applied, offer case studies and a suggested Pledge of Truth and Accuracy in Media Photography, and look ahead to the possible future of journalistic photography on the Internet.

Each chapter is accompanied by several "Explorations" designed to facilitate classroom discussion and to integrate into those interactions the students' own perceptions and experiences. The text cites thoughtful observations and the sometimes conflicting opinions of a number of photographers, authors, professors, and editors, and each chapter is further supplemented with stand-alone quotes from similar sources. As readers contemplate various examples throughout the chapters, answer the posed questions, and debate the conflicts, they should broaden their understanding of relevant principles and sharpen their perceptions of the implied authenticity of images in various publications, perhaps including their own.

While it is useful to consider these elements separately and in sequence, certain fundamental questions recur throughout the book: What is journalism? What does a photo mean? At what point does "enhancement" become "fictionalizing"? Although the guidelines offered here may be applied to media ranging from satellite news broadcasts to net-based magazines, they are rooted in print photography, whose practitioners have long grappled with the ethics of visual media and whose principles remain relevant.

Certainly, *Phototruth or Photofiction?* does not pretend to answer every question. Rather it offers a way of looking at the issues, a method of inquiry that helps readers to draw their own conclusions, to formulate protocols for their own publications. As we will see, reasonable minds may differ as to whether a particular alteration changes a photo's meaning, whether most viewers would be misled by this or that manipulation, or whether standards should differ among "hard news," features and the like.

But one thing is certain: The survival of visual journalism requires our recognizing we can no longer take for granted photography's seemingly inherent truthfulness. Furthermore, we must reconsider recent departures from long-held principles, and do a better job of informing and educating our readers. Let us explore the ethical dimensions of visual media in the digital age, with the goal of preserving a mode of communication that for generations has sparked the imaginations and enriched the lives of countless people around the world.

ACKNOWLEDGMENTS

Back in 1994, Tim Gleason, now Dean of the School of Journalism and Communication at the University of Oregon, engaged me in a conversation about ethics and imagery and co-wrote my first paper on the subject. I am indebted to him for setting me on an intellectual journey that has proved invigorating and fruitful. Shiela Reaves is an associate professor at the School of Journalism and Mass Communication at the University of Wisconsin, Madison, and the author of many scholarly papers on retouching photos; a pioneer in this field, she was encouraging and generous.

I am not a professional photographer, so it was with some trepidation that I began to share my concerns and views with working photojournalists at the National Press Photographers Association, the Associated Press, the Poynter Institute and elsewhere. They were not only tolerant, but also helpful and appreciative of my efforts.

Aside from the sorts of quotes and citations typically found in books such as this one, *Phototruth or Photofiction?* has benefited enormously from comments contributed by leading educators and practitioners in ethics, journalism and photography. They not only agreed to be interviewed, but also participated in a thoughtful "electronic forum"—an e-mail exchange occurring over several weeks. Throughout the book you will find their insights, sometimes woven into the text in various chapters and sometimes set apart.

These distinguished correspondents include Bill Allen, Editor of *National Geographic*; Deni Elliott, Professor in both the Department of Philosophy and the School of Journalism at the University of Montana and Director of the University's Practical Ethics Center; Janet Froelich, the Art Director of *The New York Times Magazine*; Phil Hood, a Senior Analyst with the Alliance For Converging Technologies, Toronto, Ontario; John Long, a photojournalist, Assistant Picture Editor at the *Hartford Courant* and the former President of the National Press Photographers Association and chairman of its ethics committee; Les Riess, President and Chairman of the Board, American Society of Media Photographers; professor, editor and author Fred Ritchin of New York University's Interactive Telecommunications Program; Randall Rothenberg, who has held senior editorial positions at *Wired, Esquire* and *The New York Times Magazine* and is the author of several acclaimed books and many feature articles; my great pal Bill Ryan, a poet, author, photographer, graphic designer and award-winning educator at the University of Oregon's School of Journalism and Communication; David Schonauer, Editor in Chief of *American Photo*; and journalist and teacher Bob Steele, director of the ethics program at the Poynter Institute for Media Studies.

I would especially like to single out Paul Lester, a photojournalist, a professor in the Department of Communication at California State University, Fullerton, a leader in the Visual Communication division of the Association for Education in Journalism and Mass Communication, and author of *Photojournalism, An Ethical Approach*, among other works. He offered advice and encouragement at every step of the way.

I would like to thank the individuals and organizations who gave permission to have their images reproduced in this volume. On the other hand, observant readers will note that some VIP's (Very Important Photos) are not pictured, even a few whose manipulations are discussed in depth. In most of these cases, reprint permission was refused because of the photo's "controversial" aspects or unspecified "legal problems," or simply because embarassed copyright holders felt the images reflected poor editorial decisions or an immature understanding of the digital process. In short, they didn't want readers to be reminded. Although the author pointed out that the inclusion of such images in a textbook would enlighten the next generation of media professionals (and that some manipulations were actually defended), these arguments were fruitless in several cases. Most of the key photos not included here have been published or discussed elsewhere, some of them dozens of times, and thus readers may be familiar with them. Even in their absence, these images must be acknowledged for their roles in the evolution of digital manipulation. Their existence is part of the story, illustrating the ongoing struggle in mediating truth and fiction.

I am indebted to my editors, Lisa Stracks, a good listener whose suggestions led to a restructuring of the manuscript's first incarnation, and Linda Bathgate, who picked up the torch. I'd like to express my sincere gratitude to the prepublication reviewers, whose insights improved the manuscript considerably: Michael Carlebach, University of Miami; Darcy Drew Greene, Michigan State University; D. G. Lewis, California State University, Fresno; Michael Perkins, Drake University; Jane Singer, Colorado State

University; Kimberly Sultze, St. Michael's College; David Sutherland, Syracuse University; Susan Zavoina, University of North Texas; and James D. Kelly, Southern Illinois University Carbondale. I am further indebted to Professor Kelly for his thoughtful and beautifully articulated Foreword.

Thanks also to my wife, Anne, for her unwavering support and good cheer, and to my journalism students at the University of Oregon for asking such provocative questions.

Tom Wheeler, 2002

1. "Newspaper editors are intolerant of altering spot news photos and much more tolerant of altering photo illustrations, and they have mixed reactions to altering feature photos." Prof. Shiela Reaves, "The Vulnerable Image: Categorization of Photo Types As Predictor of Digital Manipulation," a paper presented to the Vis. Comm. Div., AEJMC annual convention, August 1992. See also, Reaves, "Digital Alteration of Photographs in Magazines: An Examination of the Ethics," *Journal of Mass Media Ethics*, No. 3 (1991): 175.

I

A History of "Phototruth"

Chapter 1

"A Picture of Reality"
Qualified Objectivity in Visual Journalism

Soon [after its invention] the photograph was considered incontestable proof of an event, experience, or state of being.

—*The Concise Columbia Encyclopedia*[1]

COMPELLING REFLECTIONS

Any discussion of "manipulated" photography must begin with the recognition that photography itself is an inherent manipulation—a manipulation of light, a process with many steps and stages, all subject to the biases and interpretations of the photographer, printer, editor, or viewer. Photography is not absolute "reality." It is not unqualified "truth." It is not purely "objective." It was never any of those things, and it has been subject to distortion since its inception. Indeed, many of its earliest practitioners were more concerned with concocting fantasy than documenting reality. They were artists, not journalists.

Still, throughout the century and a half of its existence, one branch of photography—the sometimes loosely defined "photojournalism"—has acquired a special standing in the public mind, a confidence that a photo can *reflect* reality in a uniquely compelling and credible way.[2] Indeed, public faith in the veracity of photography is almost as old as photography itself. In *The Origins of Photojournalism in America*, Michael Carlebach explains that even in the days when photographs were typically recast as woodcuts or steel engravings prior to printing, viewers recognized their basis in photographic processes and regarded them as reliable depictions of actual events.[3]

From the 1850s throughout the Victorian era, realistic images were viewed with the wildly popular stereograph, a handheld viewer whose side-by-side photographs approximated a three-dimensional effect. Though now

> From the moment Talbot announced his new invention in 1839, the world was entranced with photography. Talbot himself realized that . . . he could freeze the visual spectacle of the world and create an object that could be savored long after the event had transpired. He could transform life into art.
> — Commentary accompanying William Henry Fox Talbot's 1843 photo "The Boulevards of Paris"[4]

considered amusing antiques or mere novelties, for half a century these devices provided to countless viewers compelling visual information about an expanding nation—its scenic wonders, architecture, political and sporting events, natural disasters, and so on. The mid-20th century saw the rise of photojournalism, as exemplified by pioneering documentary photographer Alfred Eisenstaedt. His goal: "to find and catch the storytelling moment."[5] By World War II, "America had become a certifiably visual, predominantly photographic culture."[6] Even beyond photojournalism per se, the inherent believability of photography has continued to exceed that of the printed or spoken word, as evidenced in our once-comfortable pairing of the words "photographic" and "proof," and even in openly cynical phrases such as "believe half of what you see and none of what you hear."

But why? Why has photography seemed so inherently realistic for so long? Much of the faith in mass-media imagery comes from average citizens' everyday experiences with personal photography. We point our cameras at our families, friends, and vacation sights, and view the prints as legitimate documents that "capture" the events and scenes in meaningful ways. Countless millions of us collect our photos in albums and pass them on to future generations, not only for entertainment or curiosity value but as evidence—proof of the way we once looked and the way the world once worked. As Dartmouth College professor Marianne Hirsch has said, "People say if there was a fire, the first thing they would save is their photo albums. We almost fear we'll lose our memories if we lose our albums."[7]

"PHOTOTRUTH": A KIND OF REALITY

Arguments that photography is or is not "real" seem to take for granted the idea that reality itself is purely objective. Perhaps a more enlightened view recognizes photography's inherent subjectivity as well as its undeniable potential for authenticity and resonance. As Richard Lacayo wrote in the June 8, 1998, issue of *Time*:

> Photography not only provided this century with two of the things it likes best—greater realism and superior fantasies—but also showed how deeply entwined they can be. . . . Of the pleasures cameras give us, the transfiguration

> Photography's capacity for capturing and preserving realistic images of family members, homesteads, and exotic places did much more than provide a historical record or low-cost substitute for hand-painted portraits and landscape art. It contributed to a rapid change in the way people viewed the world and enjoyed their leisure time. People soon discovered that photographic images could reveal hidden truths, such as the horrors of war, as well as create grand illusions, such as the pristine views of a virgin, "uninhabited" western frontier ready for development.
>
> — Roger Fidler, Mediamorphosis[8]

of plain reality is the most indispensable. It implies that the world is more than it seems—which, after all, it may well be. It's a paradox too lovely to ignore and too profound to solve.[9]

Because photography has never been entirely unbiased, some critics may dismiss its objective qualities altogether. But despite its subjective aspects and its history of occasional manipulation, most people have considered misleading or distorted photos to be the exceptions, as evidenced by their use of common qualifiers such as "special effects," "staged," "doctored," or "trick" photography. Readers already know, for example, that photographers or their subjects are capable of deception, that reality is not literally black and white, and that a whole world exists outside the frame of a photograph. But none of these facts have interfered with average readers' basic faith in, say, a black-and-white photo's ability to reflect aspects of the real world in revealing ways.[10] After all, "phototruth" is not based on a reader's conviction that photography *is* reality. Rather, a photograph can be true in the way a sentence can be true. Viewers will believe in its truth as long as they believe it *corresponds* in a meaningful way to reality.

This correspondence is at the core of our discussion, just as the relationship between actual events and reports of those events is essential to any discussion of journalistic authenticity. In a PBS program, Bill Moyers suggested that "one purpose of journalism is to give us a picture of reality."[11] Notwithstanding reality's many layers and ambiguity, seasoned professionals such as Moyers and laypeople alike routinely think of journalistic photography as "real" or as "a picture of reality."[12] Just a few examples:

- In a letter to *Time*, the president of the National Press Photographers Association wrote that documentary photos derive their power from "the reality they show us."[13]
- Commenting on a controversial photo manipulation, *Newsweek* assistant managing editor Mark Whitaker explained: "What makes a news photo distinctive is the fact that it is real."[14]

> [During World War II] people would not trust eyewitness accounts of the concentration camps until confronted with the photographs.
>
> — Life, Spring 1999[15]

- In *National Geographic*'s April 1998 issue, the editor explained the magazine's fundamental photo processing guideline: "Do not alter reality on the finished image."

TO FREEZE THE VISUAL SPECTACLE OF THE WORLD: MILESTONES IN THE INVENTION OF PHOTOGRAPHY

Another reason for the long-held faith in photocredibility is that photography has been perfectly suited to the science, the industry, and the obsession with "progress" so characteristic of the 20th century. Despite the all-too-human aspects of choosing subjects, framing them, and selecting only a few photos from a great many, photography's dependence on mechanical devices and chemical processes seemed to isolate it from interpretation and infuse it with some level of detachment and impartiality.

As far back as 1565 it was observed that certain silver salts turn black when exposed to the air. In the mid-1720s it was proved that this phenomenon is actually caused by exposure to light, a discovery that led to many unsuccessful attempts at capturing images in a permanent, photochemical form. The harnessing of light to fix enduring images upon light-sensitive plates, films, or papers was fervently pursued early in the 19th century not only by scientists but also by amateur inventors, painters, and other artists, some working in concert and others independently.

French scientist Joseph Nicéphore Niépce made the first paper negative in 1816. Three years later, English astronomer Sir John Herschel discovered a chemical fixing agent; he was later credited with conceiving the terms "positive," "negative," and "photography," after Niépce produced what some historians consider the first photograph, on metal, in 1827. (Some historians fix the date at 1826; others assert that too many people worked independently on similar processes to support any claims of a "first photograph.")

In 1839, Niépce's process was perfected by his partner, French stage designer and painter Louis Daguerre (1789–1851). The new "daguerreotype" allowed a positive image to be etched upon a highly polished copper plate that was coated with silver and exposed to iodine fumes (Figure 1.1). Another cornerstone was a process that permitted the printing of paper positives from a silver iodide and silver nitrate-treated paper negative called the "calotype," developed in 1841 by Englishman William Henry Fox Talbot (1800–1877), who worked at about the same time as Daguerre. His method was the first

FIGURE 1.1. Remarkable visual detail was provided by even the earliest methods of photography. This daguerreotype, an overview of a Parisian street scene, was made by Louis Daguerre himself and dates to the dawn of photography in 1839.

example of contact printing, or producing on light-sensitive paper a positive image from an original negative.

Glass, or "collodion," negatives were coated with a film of cotton dissolved in an ether/alcohol solution, then treated with salts and exposed while still wet. In 1851 Englishman Frederick Scott Archer developed this "wet plate" process, which permitted an unlimited number of prints to be made from highly detailed negatives; by 1860 it had almost completely replaced both the daguerreotype and Talbot's paper calotype. The 8,000 or so remarkably clear and detailed Civil War photos taken by Mathew Brady and his associates typically used the wet plate process (Figure 1.2). Over the next three decades various inventors experimented with the more convenient "dry plate" technique perfected in 1878.

Early salted-paper prints treated with arrowroot or other starches had a textured matte finish with a soft, atmospheric quality, while waxed-paper negatives facilitated sharper detail. From the mid-1850s almost to the turn of the century, processing was dominated by the finely detailed albumen

FIGURE 1.2. The Civil War broke out scarcely two decades after the invention of photography, yet the photos from that era are considered among the most compelling war images of all time. Mathew Brady took many photos and hired up to 100 associates to take thousands more. Union General Joseph "Fighting Joe" Hooker (1814–1879), a veteran of Manassas, Antietam, and Fredericksburg, is pictured here.

> I would willingly exchange every single painting of Christ for one snapshot.
>
> — George Bernard Shaw[16]

print, typically made from glass negatives. In this process, developed by Louis Désiré Banquart-Evrard, a sheet of paper was coated with silver salts suspended in egg whites, then exposed to sunlight through a negative. Many glossy albumen prints were given a purplish tinge by being toned with a gold chloride solution.

Developed in 1873, the platinum technique used platinum salts and light-sensitive iron salts; in this process the image was actually absorbed into the paper's fibers rather than resting on its surface. Softer than coated-paper photos, platinum prints typically had charcoal tones and deep, rich blacks. The process was popular until about 1920, along with the similar and less expensive palladium technique.

Over the last 80 years, the most common black-and-white printing technique has been a refinement of Talbot's original process, which dates back to the dawn of photography itself. In this "gelatin silver" technique, a sheet of paper is coated with a mixture of white pigment and gelatin, then with a gelatin/silver-salts solution. It is exposed to light through a negative and developed in a chemical solution.

Other milestones included the light-mixing experiments of Scottish physicist James Clerk Maxwell in 1861, which paved the way for the development of color photography; the invention in 1884 of the forerunner of modern film by American industrialist George Eastman, founder of Kodak and sometimes called the father of photography as a mass medium; and the development of the halftone process, which by 1910 had spawned a sudden and drastic increase in newspaper photography.

In *The Politics of Pictures*, John Hartley declared, "Because of its photochemical, optical and physical complexities, photography is often claimed as a product of science, but the claim is unfounded. It was a product of amateur inspiration, artistic flair and commercial showmanship, and science came limping along behind, trying to work out what was going on."[17]

However one interprets its origins, photography's effects were revolutionary, providing new ways to learn (Figure 1.3), new ways to see the world, new ways to imagine one's own life.

SUMMARY

It is hard to overstate photography's impact. As *U.S. News & World Report* concluded in 2001, "The sciences, the arts, politics, history—all were transformed. . . . the invention of photography was in itself a defining moment, a time when the world shifted. . . ."[18] Faith in photography's authenticity is

FIGURE 1.3. "Train Wreck on the Providence & Worcester Railroad," a daguerreotype by L. Wright taken on August 12, 1853. Such images provided a "you are there" realism that a century and a half later remains the cornerstone of nonfiction photography's power and credibility.

> Newsweek described America's position in the [1999] Balkan crisis as "poorly thought-out policy rescued by images of human misery." News and documentary photographers are still essential in helping us understand the impact of events big and small.
>
> — David Schonauer, American Photo[19]

almost as old as photography itself, due to chemical and mechanical aspects that seem to impart intrinsic objectivity, readers' long exposure to responsible photojournalism, and average citizens' dependence on photos as reliable documentation of their own lives. The convictions at the very foundation of photography's credibility are reflected in the use of the words "real" and "reality" by professionals and media consumers alike when distinguishing legitimate nonfiction photography from "doctored," "trick," or otherwise misleading manipulations.

Among the questions posed in later chapters are: What does a photograph mean? When is a photograph no longer real? When does an alteration go beyond mere technical enhancement and change the content or meaning of a photo? At what point does an alteration cross the line from ethical to unethical? The answers all derive from a single consideration: the public's perception of the relationship between an ostensibly journalistic image and reality. Any erosion of confidence in that relationship threatens the very existence of photography as a means of conveying nonfiction information. Later chapters explore that relationship in depth.

EXPLORATIONS

1. What kind of correspondence to reality do you think readers expect from a photograph (a) on the front page of your local newspaper, (b) on the cover of a typical national news magazine, or (c) on the cover of a consumer magazine such as *Men's Journal* or *Vogue*? Is your answer the same in every case? Why or why not?

2. Think of your own experiences with photography. Have you ever kept a photo for a long time, perhaps carried it in your purse or wallet? If so, why? Why do people keep photos of their friends, sweethearts, families, travel destinations, and so on, sometimes for many years? What kind of correspondence to actual events and scenes do such photos have? If you could keep only a few of your belongings, how much priority would you give to certain photos? Why?

3. How does the "phototruth" of your personal photos compare to images used in advertising? To images appearing in newspapers and news magazines? In general interest magazines?

> [Photojournalism] aimed to stop us and focus us, bringing us into the now, face to face with reality. Some images showed us a side of ourselves that we undervalue — the businessman in a suit and tie, riding a shopping cart in a momentary burst of childlike playfulness. Others that remain memorable — the murdered child, the young bride, the old man staring into death's eyes — are about life's most important events.
> — Phil Hood, Alliance for Converging Technologies[20]

4. Have you ever attended an event that was covered in the newspaper, such as a political rally, parade, concert, speech, or sporting event? How did your recollection of the experience compare to the news reports and photos of the event?

ENDNOTES

1. *The Concise Columbia Encyclopedia* (licensed from Columbia University Press), on CD-ROM, Microsoft Bookshelf '94, 1994; see also *The Cowles Comprehensive Encyclopedia*, Cowles Educational Books Inc., New York, 1966.
2. "By photographic realism, then, we mean something limited, although very powerful: the photograph's unmatched ability to record visible facts such as shape, texture, contour, the relationship of parts to each other and to the whole. This, indeed, photography does faster, with greater fidelity and in more minute detail, than any other medium." Arthur Goldsmith, "Photos Always Lied," *Popular Photography* (November 1991): 68.
3. Michael L. Carlebach, *The Origins of Photojournalism in America* (Washington and London: Smithsonian Institution Press, 1992), 3.
4. On display at the National Gallery of Art, Washington, D.C., June 1999.
5. *Life* (spring 1999): 8.
6. *Life* (spring 1999): 14.
7. Emily Sohn, "Want a Memory? Say 'Cheese,' " *U.S. News & World Report* (July 9–16, 2001): 71.
8. Roger Fidler, *Mediamorphosis: Understanding New Media* (Thousand Oaks, CA: Pine Forge Press, 1997), 93–94.
9. Richard Lacayo, "Camera Ready," *Time* (June 8, 1998): 88.
10. As author and educator Fred Ritchin has said, "There's a difference between an honest interpretation of an event, which any news photographer will do—for example, an attempt to report, an attempt to be a credible witness, an attempt to do the right thing, to interpret it as best they can—versus somebody who's there to manipulate, to distort, so that the reader is fooled." Janet Abrams, "Little Photoshop of Horrors: The Ethics of Manipulating Journalistic Imagery," *Print* (November/December 1995): 27.
11. "Consuming Images," *The Public Mind: Image and Reality in America* (PBS video, 1989).
12. Regarding its controversial Nancy Kerrigan/Tonya Harding composite (Chapters 4, 16), *Newsday*'s Anthony Marro said, "I have to admit, when I picked up the paper on my front porch, I said, 'Uh-oh, it looked very real.' " William Glaberson, "*Newsday* Imagines an Event, and Sets Off a Debate," *The New York Times* (February 17, 1994): A12. Another enlightening reference to the link between journalism, photography and reality appears in the official rules of the 2001–2002 William Randolph Hearst Foundation Journalism Awards Program: "This contest is journalism. Images must be real, not false. They cannot be altered digitally or in any other way that changes the content. . . . It is NOT permissible to alter the basic reality of a photograph."
13. Letters, *Time* (July 18, 1994): 5.

14. "Photo Flap: Time's Altered Image Sparks Ethics Debate," *The Phoenix Gazette* (June 22, 1994): A2.
15. *Life* (spring 1999): 14.
16. Quoted in Paul Lester, *Visual Communication: Images with Messages* (Belmont, CA: Wadsworth, 1995), 246.
17. John Hartley, *The Politics of Pictures: The Creation of the Public in the Age of Popular Media* (London: Routledge, 1992), 55.
18. Sara Sklaroff, "The Timeless Moment," *U.S. News & World Report* (July 9–16, 2001): 24.
19. David Schonauer, "In Camera" column, *American Photo* (July/August, 1999): 32.
20. Phil Hood is a senior analyst for the Alliance for Converging Technologies, Toronto, Ontario. From an interview with the author, January 1999.

Chapter 2

Old-Fashioned Fakery

Photo Manipulation in the Pre-Digital Era

Stage-managed and composite photographic techniques were common contrivances by the turn of the [20th] century.

—Paul Lester[1]

CONCOCTED REALITIES AT THE DAWN OF PHOTOGRAPHY

Photos were faked long before the development of imaging software. In fact, the first counterfeit appeared within a year of the invention of photography itself. Working independently of Louis Daguerre (Chapter 1), Frenchman Hippolyte Bayard discovered a viable photographic process on his own, rendering positive images on paper. When his early efforts went unrewarded, he made a self-portrait, supposedly of his suicide ("Portrait of the Photographer as a Drowned Man, 1840"), to protest what he considered an unfair lack of recognition by the public and government officials.

In fact, documenting reality was the furthest thing from the minds of many early photographers. Some were interested in using the miraculous new process to conjure dreams, nightmares, erotic flights of fancy, idyllic utopias, or other imaginary scenes. Even those who photographed nature, actual objects, and real people often touched up the photos, not to mislead viewers, necessarily, but simply because the notion of objective photojournalism had yet to take hold. For example, John Moran's remarkably detailed albumen print "The Wissahickon Creek near Philadelphia," from about 1865, was delicately retouched to remove the corner of a building that had intruded upon the scene (Figure 2.1). Other early examples of altered photos ranged from artistic creations to purportedly realistic scenes and portraits:

- Oscar Rejlander's "Street urchins tossing chestnuts," 1857, in which an airborne chestnut is in fact hung by an unseen thread
- Rejlander's allegorical "The Two Ways of Life," 1857, a single image that entailed combining some thirty separate negatives (Figure 2.2)

FIGURE 2.1. Many early photos were "manipulated" to make the composition more artful. In John Moran's "The Wissahickon Creek near Philadelphia," the corner of an obtrusive building was eradicated in the lab.

FIGURE 2.2. Oscar Rejlander's "The Two Ways of Life," 1857, combined some thirty separate negatives to produce what might be called a photo-allegory.

- Henry Robinson's "Fading Away," a five-negative deathbed tableaux
- Rejlander's "Hard Times," 1860, one of his "spiritistical" images intended to depict metaphysical experiences, even visits from beyond the grave
- several faked Civil War photos, including two from 1863 by Alexander Gardner that purportedly picture Confederate and Union soldiers but in fact picture one body in two poses
- "The Harvest of Death—Gettysburg, July 4, 1863," a Gettysburg battlefield engraving that is actually a composite made from three photographs (Figure 2.3). One of these photographs is yet another reproduction of Gardner's versatile Confederate/Union soldier
- a Mathew Brady photo of General Sherman's staff that was later augmented with a separate image of a general who had missed the original photo shoot
- a famous portrait of Abraham Lincoln that is actually a composite of The Great Emancipator's head atop the body of statesman John Calhoun.[2]

Also popular were "spirit photographs"—double exposures supposedly revealing the images of ghosts. Such pictures were sometimes executed by

FIGURE 2.3. "The Harvest of Death—Gettysburg, July 4, 1863" by Alexander Gardner is actually a composite made from three negatives, one of which pictures a body that the photographer used in several other photos.

> Perhaps we would be better off if journalists were more honest with themselves and with the public on the nature of photography as documentary evidence. Maybe we can learn something from the ongoing debate about "objectivity" as it applies to all forms of reporting, whether it be interviews, observations, written stories, or whatever.
>
> — Bob Steele, The Poynter Institute[3]

having a sheet-draped model appear before the lens during only a fraction of the long exposure time. Elsie Wright and Frances Griffiths, two English girls, concocted a photograph that in 1917 "captured" elves and fairies cavorting in an idyllic wood; the image remained plausible to many viewers for several decades.[4] Even "morphing," a technique typically associated with high-tech graphic software, has roots in practices and theories dating back a century or more.[5]

ENGRAVINGS AND OTHER ARTWORKS

Today we often hear of how dazzling technologies have fostered new ways of altering photos. But a century ago, it was technology's limitations that led to altered mass-media images. Many published pictures were engravings, and artists were accustomed to taking liberties in rendering them in aesthetically pleasing and dramatic ways. Photos fulfilled a subservient, prepublication role as mere references for engravers. When halftone processes sparked the publication of actual photographs on a large scale, publishers sometimes treated them as being as malleable and subject to artistic license as engravings had been.

At the dawn of the 20th century, posed photos, composites, re-enactments, and highly retouched images all were common. Examples included Edward

> It is actually a positive occurrence for the public to lose its naive view of the truth in photographs. Critical thinking is the result. In no other profession are the complaints about its practices made so public as in journalism. Consequently, the public learns to question what they see and read in all media—to not accept the company or political spin. Teach truth, practice truth, but realize that truth is as fleeting as a wet spot on a desert stone.
>
> —Paul Lester, California State University, Fullerton[6]

Steichen's 1902 composite of Rodin alongside one of his sculptures, photos of the 1906 San Francisco earthquake that were retouched to hide the extent of the devastation, and many posed and re-enacted scenes from the Spanish-American War in Cuba.

In the 1920s and 1930s, some fabricated images were the results of particularly outrageous shenanigans. Hearst art director Charlie Tebbs photographed a drunk who had passed out; in the darkroom, he painted eyeballs over the man's closed lids and unrumpled his hair to produce "a nicely posed picture." The legendary New York crime photographer Arthur Fellig (nicknamed Weegee) once explained that if he had a photo of two handcuffed criminals, he could cut the print in two and sell each half for five dollars.[7]

COMPOSOGRAPHS

The Evening Graphic newspaper of the 1920s not only staged photos but cultivated a reputation for doing so. As photojournalist and educator Ken Kobre explained, "[They] needed neither Photoshop nor computers to re-create reality when there were no photographs to accompany a story."[8]

In one notorious legal case, a man named Kip Rhinelander went to court to annul his marriage to Alice Jones on the bizarre grounds that when they had wed, he had not known she was black or of mixed race. At the request

FIGURE 2.4. This "Composograph" purported to picture a principal figure in a highly publicized annulment trial but in fact was assembled by The Evening Graphic from photos of a showgirl and various Graphic staff members.

FIGURE 2.5. Thousands of photos were heavily manipulated before publication by the Soviet government during the Communist era. In this example, Leon Trotsky and other prominent Bolsheviks were eliminated from a 1919 photo of Vladimir Lenin in Red Square.

of her lawyer, Jones stripped to the waist to prove to the court that Rhinelander should have been aware of her race. Photographers were barred from the proceedings, but *The Evening Graphic*'s assistant art director collected 20 photographs, including an image of a showgirl who posed as Jones might have appeared in court; *Graphic* staff members posed as other trial participants. Fragments of these images were then assembled into a cut-and-paste concoction that became known as a "composograph" (Figure 2.4). (The assistant art director is said to have grumbled, "Hell with photographers, what we need 'em for?") The publication of what seemed to be a photo of the semi-nude Alice Jones in court caused a sensation. *The Graphic*'s circulation promptly rose from 60,000 to several hundred thousand.[9]

When Rudolph Valentino's widow claimed after a seance that the silent film sensation had met legendary singer Enrico Caruso in heaven, a composograph "documented" the event.[10] In the *Graphic*'s "Photo Drama from Life" section, actors re-created news stories (or made them up); these multi-panel photographic series had irresistible if shameful titles, such as "Cripple Drowns Attempting to Rescue Madwoman." Sometimes the composographs combined drawings and photos, as in one image of an exorcist casting out a demon.[11] In another outlandish example, the *Graphic*'s managing editor hired a man and a woman, dressed them in pajamas, and pasted on their photos the faces of "Daddy" Edward Browning and his teenaged bride, Peaches, who were then engaged in a sensationalized annulment trial.

FIGURE 2.5. Continued. Manipulated version.

Browning was supposedly berating the half-clad Peaches for refusing to prance about their bedroom naked.

NOW YOU SEE HIM . . .

Most or all of the 20th century's political dictatorships faked photos for propaganda purposes, portraying leaders as more youthful, athletic, benevolent or popular than they really were, or eliminating officials who had fallen out of favor. For instance, Leon Trotsky and other principals in the Bolshevik Revolution were painted out of a November 1919 photo of Vladimir Lenin in Red Square (Figure 2.5). Many such examples are detailed in David King's 1997 book *The Commissar Vanishes: The Falsification of Photographs and Art in Stalin's Russia* (New York: Metropolitan/Henry Holt), and in Alain Jaubert's *Making People Disappear: An Amazing Chronicle of Photographic Deception* (Washington, D.C.: Pergamon-Brassey's International Defense Publishers, 1986).

"HILLARY CLINTON ADOPTS ALIEN BABY (OFFICIAL PHOTO!)"

Decades before the *Weekly World News* published articles with titles such as "Hillary Clinton Adopts Alien Baby (Official Photo!)," various hoaxes were foisted upon the public using darkroom trickery in magazine and newspaper images. Such hoaxes include a "photo" of kids playing with a wishbone as

> Readers might be shocked to see the extraordinary numbers of photos that have been retouched over time by newspaper retouchers, so that people in the frame have been removed. Not just the Kremlin did this. [American] newspapers did this routinely. They took out extraneous people.
> —Janet Froelich, The New York Times Magazine[12]

big as a tree limb, supposedly from a colossal turkey; and the faked April Fool's Day 1933 collapse of Wisconsin's state house dome.[13]

More serious or damaging frauds included a composite purporting to show McCarthy-era political candidate Senator Millard Tydings of Maryland conferring with a Communist official (the wrongfully disgraced candidate lost the subsequent election); a 1928 composite of Herbert Hoover and his vice-presidential candidate, faked because Hoover refused to pose with his own running mate; and a 1923 photo of three Soviet farmers that was doctored, rather poorly, and then introduced in 1991 as "evidence" that three downed airmen were still held prisoner in Vietnam.[14]

SUMMARY

Altered photography is not new. In fact, when *Life* magazine debuted in 1936, its policy against substantial retouching was considered something of a departure, because at least some mass-media photos had been staged, combined with other images, supplemented with pencils or paint, and otherwise manipulated for so long.

Despite the abundance and occasional outrageousness of such fakes, photography's basic credibility remained intact. Long before *Life*'s stated policy against manipulation, many newspapers and magazines had published countless photos that aside from conventional darkroom processing were unaltered. "Trick," "staged," and "doctored" images were all distinguished from "real" ones and were perceived to be the exceptions, not the rule. That assumption may be changing, as we will see in the next two chapters.

EXPLORATIONS

1. What do the terms "doctored," "trick," and "special-effects" photography suggest? Give examples of each. What do they all have in common? What kind of photography is distinguished from such alterations? That is, what do we call photography that is *not* subject to doctoring, tricks, or special effects?

2. In your own experience, how often do you encounter photographs that, you assume, have been substantially manipulated or even cooked up from scratch? Do you seem to encounter them more often than you used to? Where do you see such photos most often?

3. Bring to class examples of "doctored," "trick," or "special-effects" photography in mass media. Compare advertising images to photos used in news or other journalistic contexts (illustrating feature articles in magazines, for example). Are the images labeled in regard to their fictional content? Can you find examples when labels are necessary? Unnecessary? Why or why not?

ENDNOTES

1. Paul Lester, *Photojournalism: An Ethical Approach* (Hillsdale, NJ: Lawrence Erlbaum Assoc., 1991), 100.

2. Lester, *Photojournalism*, 91–98; see also Arthur Goldsmith, "Photos Always Lied," *Popular Photography* (November 1991): 68; Janet Abrams, "Little Photoshop of Horrors: The Ethics of Manipulating Journalistic Imagery," *Print* (November/December 1995): 24–45, 159–64.

3. Journalist and teacher Bob Steele is the director of the ethics program at the Poynter Institute for Media Studies in St. Petersburg, Florida. From an e-mail correspondence with the author, fall 1998.

4. Goldsmith, 68.

5. In the parlance of contemporary graphic artists, "morphing" refers to a computerized animation technique that renders the gradual, seamless transformation of one object or creature into another. Widely seen examples appeared in Michael Jackson's "Black or White" music video and in the feature films *Terminator 2* (featuring a humanoid robot who could take on a liquid-metal form) and *The Abyss* (with creatures whose bodies and faces consisted of water). See Tony Rimmer and Paul Lester, "Morphing, Mean Man, and Mr. Galton: Francis Galton's 1870s Photographic Work as an Early Example of Morphing," a paper presented at the annual convention of the Association for Education in Journalism and Mass Communication (AEJMC), a joint Visual Communication/History Division research session, Atlanta, August 1994.

6. Photojournalist Paul Lester is a professor in the Department of Communication at California State University, Fullerton, a leader in the visual communication division of the Association for Education in Journalism and Mass Communication, and author of *Photojournalism: An Ethical Approach*, among other works. From an e-mail correspondence with the author, fall 1998.

7. Wilson Lowrey, "Altered Plates: Photo Manipulation and the Search for News Value in the 1920s and 1990s," a paper presented to the annual convention of AEJMC, Visual Communication Division, Baltimore, MD, August 1998.

8. Ken Kobre, "The Long Tradition of Doctoring Photos," *Visual Communication Quarterly* (spring 1995): 14–15.

9. Kobre, 14–15.

10. Bob Stepno, "Staged, Faked and Mostly Naked: Photographic Innovation at the Evening Graphic (1924–1932)," a graduate student paper (School of Journalism and Mass Communication, University of North Carolina at Chapel Hill), presented to the annual convention of AEJMC, Visual Communication Division, Chicago, 1997, 3.

11. Stepno, 4.

12. Janet Froelich is the art director of *The New York Times Magazine*. "Forum Focus: Photo-journalism or Photo-fiction," a video produced by the Freedom Forum, 1101 Wilson Blvd., Arlington, Virginia 22209; 1995.

13. Lester, *Photojournalism*, 105, 106.

14. Goldsmith, 68. See also A. David Gordon and John Michael Kittross, *Controversies in Media Ethics* (New York: Longman, 1999), 281–84.

II

Implications of the New Digital Age

Chapter 3

The Digital Media Landscape

Liquid Imagery, Shaky Credibility

High-tech deception is today's technology, not tomorrow's.
—The Dallas Morning News[1]

It may be comforting to cling to old categories of photography, to assure ourselves that whatever happens outside the field of "photojournalism" will have little impact on the credibility of news photos. However, this book takes the opposite view. While our primary concern is journalistic photography, and while people do indeed bring different expectations to different media (a daily newspaper vs. a sci-fi movie, for example), public faith in "phototruth" is surely affected by everyday experiences with viewing and interpreting visual media in a variety of forms—especially considering the much-decried blurring of lines between news, public relations, advertising, and entertainment. To better grasp the threat to the credibility of still photography in newspapers and magazines, it will serve us well to briefly explore developments in broadcast television, cable, film, computer programs, personal game toys, and so on.

On occasion, this book examines even tabloids such as *National Enquirer* and satirical magazines such as *Spy*, not because they are typically included in discussions of serious journalism (obviously, they are not) but because they are part of the digital-media landscape and because the flood of photofiction from myriad sources will likely influence how viewers perceive mass-media images of all kinds—including journalistic photos.

Anybody with five minutes of Photoshop training can go in and do this. The tools are leaving the hands of journalists. We are not bringing all those years of experience to bear on what we're doing in trying to be fair and accurate, and that's what scares me.

—John Long, former president, NPPA[2]

NO GOING BACK

"The digital revolution is over," according to the November/December 1997 issue of *American Photo* magazine, and while the media's adoption of these technologies will evolve for some time, the claim that digital media are here to stay is indeed beyond debate. Professional photographers and publications embrace digital cameras and processes with increasing frequency. That same issue of *American Photo* quoted a commercial photographer as saying, "A couple of years ago I couldn't imagine what I would do with a computer; now I can't imagine what I would do without one." The magazine concluded, "The paradigm *has* shifted, and there's no going back."[3]

Most photographs seen in news magazines and newspapers with substantial circulations are either created by digital processes or converted into digital data during production.[4] What makes this ethically significant is an essential quality of digital data: its susceptibility to easy, unlimited, and virtually undetectable manipulation.

SHIFTS IN AUTHORITY

While recent discussion has understandably addressed dazzling new technologies, another factor in the new age is a shift in authority. People making decisions about how or whether images should be manipulated are increasingly part of what might be called the computer-graphics culture and are not steeped in the traditional values of photojournalism, or journalism of any kind. This is especially true of many communicators who find the Internet better suited to their tastes and goals than established print or broadcast media.[5]

Moreover, while photographers have long lamented their lack of control over how their images are published, their influence has diminished even further in recent years. Because a single image can be fragmented into components more easily than ever (the beach, the palm tree, and the moon can be isolated, sold to separate clients, and perhaps later recombined in different ways), the notion of ownership of a photo faces redefinition; some observers suggest it is already outdated.[6] One complicating factor is the Internet, which has made it almost effortless to steal, reproduce, and redistribute copyrighted material—text and images alike.[7]

IS A PHOTO "WHATEVER YOU WANT IT TO BE"?

Even the word "photograph" itself may be on its way to the boneyard of outmoded concepts. Nature photographer Art Wolfe is well known for his "photo" of a zebra herd, some members of which were digitally cloned (Figure 3.1). He said in 1997, "For me, making a digital photo is like making a watercolor. . . . It's not a painting, and it's not a photo. It's something altogether new."[8] Professor Shiela Reaves reported that the Meredith Corporation's director of production told magazine educators, "I don't consider a photograph to be a photograph anymore. It's something to work with."[9]

Indeed, once a digital image has been altered, the altered version becomes, in a very real sense, the new "original." Roger Ressmeyer sold a photo that was subsequently altered. "People want the altered image, and I don't have it," he reported. "My original is worthless."[10]

However we might define a photograph today, most of us have grown up thinking of a photo as being more fixed, more tangible, more *real* than merely "something to work with." Is the Meredith Corporation production director's quote a glimpse of things to come? Is a photograph no longer a photograph? Is it instead, as Kodak's 1996 advertising slogan promised, "whatever you want it to be"?

FIGURE 3.1. When is a photo not a photo? Art Wolfe is well known for this image of a herd of zebras, some of which were digitally cloned. Describing the process of making a digital photo, he said, "It's not a painting, and it's not a photo. It's something altogether new."

Film will continue to dominate in advertising, fashion, landscape and fine art photography. As far as print photojournalism is concerned, however, we are entering the last days of film as the primary acquisition medium. Major newspapers and wire services have already made the conversion to digital. News magazines are fighting a rear guard action to continue the use of film, but it is inevitable that the issues of time and immediacy, in all media, will eventually force them to make the move to digital. Soon, the only photographers who will be using film are those working on long-term essays, or on assignment in remote areas of the world.

— Dirck Halstead, The Digital Journalist[11]

CHANGING ASSUMPTIONS

Larger questions abound. What is the future of photographic credibility and, by extension, the credibility of all visual media, in an age when even amateur shutterbugs have access to increasingly affordable digital cameras (from 1995 to 1997, sales of these items increased by about 700 percent) and to software designed for, as one 1997 advertisement put it, "everything from retouching pimples to removing an ex-spouse"? Signposts in the digital landscape:

- In the wake of the September 11, 2001, terrorist attacks in New York and Washington, D.C., actor/director Ben Stiller ordered the digital erasing of the World Trade Center towers from scenes of Manhattan's skyline in his film *Zoolander*.
- Aki, the digitally animated female protagonist of the sci-fi movie *Final Fantasy*, was selected over real-life models and starlets to become the cover girl for *Maxim* magazine's "Hot 100" supplement in 2001.
- During the 2001 elections in Britain, the Labor Party associated their opponent, William Hague, with Margaret Thatcher by distributing composite posters that pictured Hague's face with Ms. Thatcher's hair and earrings.
- Telecommunications giant Alcatel produced a TV ad in 2001 that used footage of Martin Luther King Jr.'s famous "I have a dream" speech. A portion of the doctored version (in vintage black & white, complete with authentic looking scratches and flecks) seemed to show Dr. King speaking not to the familiar teeming throng but rather to a deserted Washington Mall.
- At the 2002 Winter Olympic Games in Salt Lake City, downhill skiers raced against the clock, one at a time; with new synchronized replay technology, broadcasters later superimposed "ghost" images of two competitors so viewers could compare their progress at various stages of their respective runs.

- During speed skating events in the 2002 Winter Olympic Games, the nationalities of competitors were identified by flags digitally inserted beneath the ice in their respective lanes. Two years previously, digital flags on the bottom of the pool identified the nationalities of Olympic swimmers; the technology is so sophisticated that one could see surface waves and shimmering reflections above the flags.
- *The New York Times* reported in 2000 that fictional websites were increasingly popular. Some offer no actual services or products but are graphically indistinguishable from those that do.
- Webbie Tookay posed for a feature in the October 1999 *Details* magazine, pitched Nokia telephones to Latin American consumers, and was slated to join a virtual band; the digital creation of animator Steven Stahlberg, Tookay is "managed" by the Illusion 2K agency, which represents virtual models.
- Yearbook photos are sometimes manipulated by students (or their parents). Aside from cosmetic touch-ups to photos of themselves, a photographer's representative said in 1999 that customers view photos of other people, then say, "I like that smile, that pose, that background or those clothes." Aspects of these details can be incorporated into the customer's own "portrait."[12]
- Hewlett Packard encourages its software customers to "crop and manipulate images—all as creativity dictates."
- Tiger Electronics introduced the Clone Zone and Dear Diary "electronic organizers," boasting that "kids can even morph the photos!"
- With Mattel's Me2Cam digital video camera/CD Rom system, a child "can actually step into the computer"; its features include a "virtual fun house that distorts her image!"
- Software now permits computer operators to add images of new products into old film or live video feeds. Stars in classic movies from bygone eras could appear to be holding or using the latest brand-name products. Signs, billboards or other commercial messages could also be integrated, the results looking as if the inserts had been part of the original scene. In one remarkable example of "virtual advertising," a Blockbuster videocassette box was digitally placed on a table in an episode of the "Seven Days" television series.[13] The March 17,

---

It was true that there was no such person as Comrade Oglivy, but a few lines of print and a couple of faked photographs would soon bring him into existence. . . . Comrade Oglivy, who had never existed in the present, now existed in the past, and when once the act of forgery was forgotten, he would exist just as authentically, and upon the same evidence, as Charlemagne or Julius Caesar.

— George Orwell, 1984

We're already making biographical historical films now, like Nixon . . . but instead of an actor to portray Nixon, we could have it appear that Nixon himself plays the part. People will say, "We're going to be lied to!" But we're already lied to. It's a matter of degree.

— Mark Dippé, film director[14]

1999, episode of that series featured the live-video insertion of "electronic product images" for Coca-Cola, Wells Fargo, and other sponsors in background scenes.

- Syndicators of the television show *Law and Order* announced in 2001 they were working on agreements to provide post-production insertion of images of logos, signs, and products into previously filmed scenes. Payments would be in addition to fees advertisers paid for regular ads. A spokesman for Princeton Video Image (PVI) said, "You could sell a box of cereal in the kitchen one [airing], and dish soap in the next." PVI's website explains that the distribution of these "virtual insertions" could also be allocated by region: "For example, the sitcom *Frasier* can have a can of Coke on his living room table in the Northeast region broadcasts, and a can of Diet Coke on his living room table for the West Coast broadcast region. A broadcaster can show a *Seinfeld* rerun with a box of Corn Flakes on Jerry's kitchen table one time and a box of Special K the next time the show aired."
- Racing cars are typically plastered with sponsors' logos, but during portions of the Fox Sports Network broadcast of NASCAR's 2001 Budweiser Shootout, some vehicles looked oddly blank; the network had digitally removed the logos from some of the cars whose advertisers had failed to pay Fox for displaying them.
- With DivorceX software from Canada's Western Pro Imaging Labs, "divorcees can now eradicate their previous partners from photographs without resorting to a scissor job. . . . The technology can also make people thinner, younger, and can remove double chins or scars."
- Do-it-yourself photo portrait booths offer the option of "Foto Fantasy" digital manipulation.
- Kai's Photo Soap software permits amateur photographers to fix their pictures by, among other alterations, removing objects in the background.
- Kodak's Image Magic theater kiosks let moviegoers create digital posters of their "appearances" in Hollywood films.
- Introduced in 1998, the Game Boy Camera costs only $49, is marketed to kids, and invites users to "take snapshots of your friends . . . and make them a part of the action as their faces become the characters."

There may be nothing unethical about these practices, but can even newspaper photography maintain its authenticity in a visual environment where viewers are bombarded with images in which fanciful dreamscapes appear to be as real as any photograph, humans are "morphed" into phantasms, and dead celebrities come back to life to mingle with contemporary actors, to hawk beer, to dance with vacuum cleaners?[15]

DECLINING CONFIDENCE

We may even be approaching a time when the public will assume that unless otherwise specified a journalistic photo is *likely* to have been altered. In the aftermath of its highly controversial—and highly altered—1994 O.J. Simpson cover (addressed in the next chapter), *Time*'s managing editor felt compelled to assure readers that certain other photos in the magazine had *not* been altered.[16] The statement was among the most revealing of the many comments made in the wake of the Simpson debacle; previously, no such promises had been deemed necessary in the venerable news magazine.

The implications of increasing photofakery are particularly significant in light of a declining confidence in journalism itself. *Newsweek*'s July 20, 1998, issue reported, "The public's faith in the press may be at a new low,"[17] and in September 1998 the *American Journalism Review* devoted several feature articles to recent, highly publicized ethical lapses.[18] (Even *60 Minutes* was duped into airing a phony "documentary" featuring actors, misleading locations, and staged events.[19])

Another relevant trend is visual imagery's increasing dominance over the printed word. As NYU professor and critic Neil Postman has said, "The environment created by language, and the printed word, has now been moved to the periphery of the culture . . . and at its center, the image has taken over."[20]

> The photographer who came to photograph me knew that the photograph was going to be manipulated. I said, "Do you know what is going to happen?" and he said, "No." I thought, How can you take my picture if you don't know what is going to be done with your photograph? It was a job. There was a sense that photographers had lost control of this process and a more centralized authority would make those decisions. So I really think that in many ways the day of the photographer has passed . . . what they've become is fodder for everybody else who may want to use their images.
> — Fred Ritchin, New York University[21]

> It's gotten to the point that our ability to manufacture fraud now exceeds our ability to detect it.
>
> —producer/writer Andrew Niccol[22]

BEYOND PRINT MEDIA

Our challenge extends beyond newspapers and magazines to broadcast, cable, film, video, and online media. All of the image-manipulation techniques available to print media have analogs in digital video and film editing,[23] providing new opportunities not only to Hollywood studios but also to news organizations—or for that matter anyone with access to a digital camera and a computer. On a wintry January day in 1994, bundled-up ABC television correspondent Cokie Roberts was introduced to viewers as reporting "from Capitol Hill"; in fact, she was in a presumably comfy Washington studio, standing before a projected image of the Capitol building (the network apologized).[24]

The ABC/Roberts trickery was decidedly low-tech compared to what's on the horizon. *The Dallas Morning News* reported that with the latest software, "news anchors can do their stuff on camera in a bare, blue room . . . the whole set is dubbed in digitally, to show any kind of style, scenery, furniture, you name it."[25] Producer/writer Andrew Niccol was quoted in 2001 as saying, "Very soon we will be able to turn on our television sets and not know if the presenter is real or fake, and frankly we won't care." In one example, an animated "cyber anchor" named Ananova appeared on a website to read actual news and weather reports. According to the May 7, 2001, *New York Times* (p. B8), "Within weeks after her debut last year, Ananova was besieged by requests for personal appearances, calls from Hollywood agents and record companies asking to sign her."

In his classic work, *1984*, George Orwell offered this description of the ultimate totalitarian state's propaganda mechanism: "There were the huge printing shops with their sub-editors, their typography experts, and their elaborately equipped studios for the faking of photographs." One wonders what Orwell might have thought of this 1996 announcement for Reality 3-D software (note that the product is directed not to advertisers but to news professionals):

> EarthWatch . . . introduces a revolutionary new product line. Reality 3-D is the next step in graphics, permitting real-time animations for weather and news . . . [providing] a simulated helicopter perspective with a photorealistic Virtual City Skyline. . . . The system will simulate fires, explosions, and permit the user to re-create accidents in near real-time, getting compelling visuals on the air . . . before video arrives on the scene. With a virtual set, your weather or news talent can be in a simulated 3-D landscape, walking knee-deep through fronts, storms, or hurricanes, or walking through your virtual skyline."[26]

Videographers have long been able to restructure raw footage to create new
mputer modeling, vocal sampling, and re-animation
ally put words in a speaker's mouth. The faces of
l Jack Lemmon were digitally "pasted" onto the
horseback in the film *My Fellow Americans*.[27] In
e *Phantom Menace*, nonanimated characters exist-
lm "interacted" with real actors filmed in studios
3.2); also, a live actor's expression from one take
o his face in another take.[28] The technology that
at briefly with John F. Kennedy in *Forrest Gump*
s groups decree that the public wants to see a
onardo Di Caprio opposite a teenaged Elizabeth
on be able to render it on computers.
ions of applying these technologies to a faked
, disaster announcement, or declaration of war.
will be able to get in there and manipulate
, special effects supervisor on the films *Contact*
President Clinton speaking about events in the
Who Framed Roger Rabbit? "It's going to be
of our lives."[29]
costs of video gear and easy-to-use software,
a shoestring can make reasonably professional
th special effects. Given the Internet, as well as

FIGURE 3.2. In <u>Star Wars: Episode I—The Phantom Menace</u>, digital characters seemed to interact with real people. While no one questions the ethics of such applications, some worry that the deluge of photofiction may eventually undermine photocredibility in all its forms.

an expected increase in satellite transmissions and the advent of cable modems and multiple digital television channels, those videos will soon be distributed worldwide with ease—and perhaps without whatever ethical safeguards might have been attached had they emerged through conventional channels.[30] Then again, as we will see in Chapter 19, the World Wide Web may facilitate a new kind of photo-based storytelling whose layers of meaning and richness of context are scarcely approached by traditional photojournalism.

SUMMARY

Digital technologies continue to revolutionize all mass media, not only exposing the public to more manipulated images but also giving them more opportunities to do the manipulating themselves, even in their everyday, personal photographic experiences. Some consequences of all this remain unclear, but certainly the assumption that "seeing is believing" is under as-

FIGURE 3.3. Several techniques were employed to alter an original photo (this page) of George Bush and Margaret Thatcher. What does the altered version (next page) suggest about the conversation—and perhaps the relationship—between the former heads of state?

sault. The next chapter explores how photographic practice has evolved amid this environment of elastic imagery.

EXPLORATIONS

1. The photos in Figure 3.3 show relatively simple manipulations of a photograph of George Bush and Margaret Thatcher. What does each version suggest about the conversation—and perhaps the relationship—between the former President and former Prime Minister?

2. Did you see the TV commercial of a few years ago, in which a teenage boy sits at his computer, puts angel wings on the picture of his girlfriend and e-mails it to her printer? How about the one in which the exhausted last-place distance runner alters the photo of the finish-line time clock so as to impress his friends with his own performance? What sorts of messages are conveyed by such advertisements? Is the credibility of journalistic photography affected, or is it immune from such influences?

3. Have you ever altered the content of a photograph, video image, or computer image? Under what circumstances, and using what tech-

nologies? Discuss whether the appropriateness of different levels of alteration would vary depending upon how the image was to be used.

4. What is your general opinion of the credibility of what has come to be called "the media"? Regarding the authenticity of what you see on television, for example, what distinctions, if any, do you make among the following?
   - local or national newscasts
   - news-oriented "talking head" or pundit talkfests such as *The McLaughlin Group*
   - celebrity-oriented "magazine format" reports (e.g., *Entertainment Tonight*)
   - news-oriented "magazine format" shows (*Prime Time Live!, Dateline, 48 Hours*, etc.), and
   - so-called reality-based entertainment such as *Cops* and *Survivor*

ENDNOTES

1. Jim Wright, "Movie Plot Should Dog Wags in White House," *The Dallas Morning News* (March 1, 1998): 7J.
2. An eminent commentator on altered photography, photojournalist John Long of the *Hartford Courant* is the former president of the National Press Photographers Association and chairman of its ethics committee. "Forum Focus: Photo-journalism or Photo-fiction," a video produced by the Freedom Forum, 1101 Wilson Blvd., Arlington, Virginia 22209; 1995.
3. David Schonauer, "The Future of Photography 1997," *American Photo* (November/December 1997): 47.
4. Edgar Shaohua Huang, "Readers' Perception of Digital Alteration and Truth-Value in Documentary Photographs," submitted in partial fulfillment for a Ph.D. degree, School of Journalism, Indiana University (October 1999): 2–3.
5. "Control over [the moment, composition, light, color] has been transferred from the photographer to the photo lab." Donald R. Katz, "Why Pictures Lie," *Esquire* (June 1990): 94; "These people [art directors and designers] have not been taught the traditional, classic values and goals of documentary photojournalism," George Wedding of *The Sacramento Bee* quoted in J.D. Lasica, "Photographs That Lie: The Ethical Dilemma of Digital Retouching," *Washington Journalism Review* (June 1989): 24; see also, Paul Lester, editor, "NPPA Code of Ethics," *NPPA Special Report: The Ethics of Photojournalism* (Durham, NC: National Press Photographers Association, 1990): 130–31.
6. "In the digital age, when images can be lifted from the Internet or scanned from books and magazines, the notion of copyright is simply antiquated." David Schonauer, "In Camera" column, *American Photo* (July/August 1999): 32. Some people disagree, such as members of the FPG (Freelance Photographers' Guild), which sued *Newsday* because the New York daily scanned a James Porto photo-illustration, then added, deleted, and recombined various elements, and published it without attribution or permission. *Newsday* settled out of court. *Newsday* attorney Bruce Keller said, "This is a simple copyright issue, not a new technology issue," but FPG President Barbara Roberts noted that digital technology had made the theft of images much easier. Akiko Busch, "Stock and Security: FPG vs. Newsday," *Print* (November/December 1995): 48.
7. "The ease at which written material can be copied and distributed on the Internet has made it possible to steal copyrighted works in staggering proportions." Martha L. Stone, "Copyright Questions Abound on the Web," *Editor & Publisher* (December 12, 1998): 44.
8. David Schonauer, "Showcase: Art Wolfe," *American Photo* (November/December 1997): 56.
9. Shiela Reaves, "Digital Alteration of Photographs in Magazines: An Examination of the Ethics," a paper presented at the annual convention of the Association for Education in Journalism and Mass Communication (AEJMC), Washington, D.C., August 1989, 8. See also Shiela Reaves, "Photography, Pixels, and New Technology: Is There a 'Paradigm Shift'?" a paper presented at the annual convention of AEJMC, Washington, D.C., August 1989.

10. Reaves, "Photography, Pixels," 9.

11. Dirck Halstead, "Looking Ahead to Photojournalism 2001," *The Digital Journalist*, http://digitaljournalist.org/issue9809/editorial.htm.

12. Cree Lawson (AP), "Retouching Yearbook Pictures Catches on," *The Register-Guard*, Eugene, Oregon (June 25, 1999): 11A.

13. "You are seeing the first glimpse of the future of advertising," according to a spokesman for Aegis Group P.L.C. From an advertiser's point of view, one advantage to the new strategy is that it allows updated or entirely new products to be placed in the same film or video at different times or for different audiences. Stuart Elliott, "Real or Virtual? You Call It: Digital Sleight of Hand Can Put Ads Almost Anywhere," *The New York Times* (October 1, 1999): C1.

14. Mr. Dippé formerly worked at Industrial Light & Magic. See Seiler, 5D.

15. In television commercials aired in 1997, footage from three Fred Astaire movies was combined with film of Dirt Devil products. Diet Coke ads seemed to capture Paula Abdul dancing with Gene Kelly, and Elton John performing with Louis Armstrong. Sean Means, "Altered Images: Photo Technology Creates a Reality That's Not There," *Salt Lake Tribune* (March 3, 1997): B1.

16. James R. Gaines, "To Our Readers," *Time* (July 4, 1994): 4.

17. Evan Thomas and Gregory L. Vistica, "Fallout from a Media Fiasco," *Newsweek* (July 20, 1998): 24. In addition, a July 4, 1999, Associated Press story reported the results of a telephone survey taken by Vanderbilt University's First Amendment Center. The center's ombudsman, Paul McMasters, said, "The news media is in deep trouble with the American public." AP, "Survey Indicates Public Fed Up With News Media," *The Register-Guard*, Eugene, Oregon (July 4, 1999): 5A.

18. Judith Sheppard, "Playing Defense: Is Enough Being Done To Prevent Future Journalistic Embarrassments?" *American Journalism Review* (September 1998).

19. AP, December 7, 1998.

20. "Consuming Images," *The Public Mind: Image and Reality in America* (PBS video, 1989).

21. Janet Abrams, "Little Photoshop of Horrors: The Ethics of Manipulating Journalistic Imagery," *Print* (November/December 1995): 43.

22. *The New York Times*, May 7, 2001, p. B8.

23. "Video will go the same way as film as newsrooms turn to new computer technology . . . much of the equipment and technology now exists." Lou Prato, "Coming Up: Digital Pictures at 11," *American Journalism Review* (July/August 1994): 48.

24. "Darts and Laurels" column, *Columbia Journalism Review* (May/June 1994): http://www.cjr.org/year/94/3/d_l.asp.

25. Wright, 7J. See also Prato, 48.

26. Don Fitzpatrick, "Shoptalk," Don Fitzpatrick Associates, http://www.tvspy.com, October 8, 1996.

27. See Andy Seiler, "Technology Puts Fiction in 'Contact' with Reality," *USA Today* (July 30, 1997): 5D.

28. "This may be the first step toward a cinematic future in which virtual actors replace flesh-and-blood ones. . . ." David A. Kaplan, "The Selling of Star Wars," *Newsweek* (May 17, 1999): 60.

29. Kaplan, 60.

30. Bruce Haring, "Digital Video: A Movie Star in the Making," *USA Today* (July 1, 1998): 5D.

Chapter 4

The New Threat

Digital Deception and the Loss of Faith

In the future, readers of newspapers and magazines will probably view news pictures more as illustrations than as reportage, since they can no longer distinguish between a genuine image and one that has been manipulated.

—Andy Grunberg, *The New York Times*[1]

PHOTOTRUTH—A QUAINT CONCEPT?

Photocredibility has survived despite photography's history of occasional duplicity, but the advent of digital manipulation may accomplish in short order what a century and a half of other methods of photofakery failed to effect.

More than a few commentators have observed, "There's nothing new about faking photos," but that is not quite right. There is something new. Computer technology has made photo doctoring much easier to do and accessible to many more people. New techniques entail manipulating computer-stored "pixels" (picture elements) rather than paints, masks, and so on. Objects or swatches of colors can be "picked up" and relocated or eliminated. A patch of sky or grass or even skin can be "cloned" and used as a "paintbrush" of sorts, to enlarge, reproduce, rearrange, or mask elements within the frame. Various blurring and blending tools help make manipulations undetectable.[2]

It seems that with each unveiling of a new graphics software program, with each discovery of a new processing technique, the opportunities for fictionalizing images become ever more numerous, more tempting.[3] One result, as the editors of *American Photo* claimed, is that, "the objective 'truth' of photographs has become something of a quaint concept."[4] This transformation raises thorny ethical challenges for professionals, educators, and students alike.

It may be that we have created unrealistic expectations to begin with. The photograph has always been subject to certain manipulations, but we have imbued the documentary photo with verisimilitude beyond its nature. It looked like reality so we equated it with reality. In truth, the photograph is only a two-dimensional piece of paper. . . . A photograph symbolically represents reality; it is not in itself reality."

—John Long, former president, NPPA[5]

On the January 1997 PBS program *Media Matters*, host Alex Jones explained "the classic way [photojournalism] has worked for decades," referring to photo selection, enlargement, and cropping. He added, "But the image itself was rarely tinkered with beyond that. It just wasn't possible, for instance, to seamlessly remove an unwanted person from a group shot or put one person's head on another person's body. Today's computer technology makes such alterations not only easy but undetectable. And it's happening— a lot."[6] The National Press Photographers Association's Michael Morse agreed: "People have no idea how much alteration is going on."[7]

VIEWER CONFUSION AND SUSPICION

Evidence mounts that computer-altered photography is contributing to a loss of confidence in journalism, and that media consumers are becoming confused. It has also become evident that the line between news and satire may not be as distinct as previously thought. When *Spy* magazine put an image of actress Daryl Hannah's face on the body of a model dressed the way Jackie Kennedy appeared on the day President John Kennedy was shot, a reader wrote to complain that she was "appalled" that Hannah, then John F. Kennedy Jr.'s girlfriend, "would even consider doing such a cover." The letter was published in a subsequent issue, but *Spy* editors, well known for ridiculing writers of critical letters, this time printed no reply at all.[8]

The confusion is hardly confined to consumers of satirical publications such as *Spy*. Readers of *Condé Nast Traveler* accused acclaimed photojournalist Mary Ellen Mark of digitally inserting a castle into her photo of the Bombay harbor; in fact, the castle was a reflection in a window (Figure 4.1).[9] The March 1996 *National Geographic* published Frans Lanting's photo of an Antarctic emperor penguin amid dozens of chicks. The visual contrast between the shiny-coated, colorful adult bird and the fuzzy-looking, black-and-white chicks caused *American Photo* to ask rhetorically: "Is it real or is it digital?"[10]

For decades, photojournalists and editors have conscientiously opposed misleading alterations, particularly in "hard news" photos (images of wars,

FIGURE 4.1.   Some readers assumed that the reflected image of the castle in this Mary Ellen Mark photo had been inserted with digital tools or some other trickery.

crime scenes, political events, natural disasters, etc.). As computer manipulations have entered the editorial mainstream, however, adherence to photojournalistic norms has given way to the temptations of commerce—not only in satirical or general interest publications but sometimes in respected newspapers and news magazines as well. The foremost examples involve a murder suspect at the center of one of the 20th century's most frenzied media spectacles, and an architectural wonder of the ancient world.

Time's O.J. Simpson Cover

Time magazine's June 27, 1994, cover featured a computer-retouched L.A.P.D. mug shot of O.J. Simpson; the blurred and darkened image was identified on the contents page as a "photo-illustration."[11] Many observers considered the cover to be nothing less than a misleading and perhaps racist or legally prejudicial attempt to make the former football star, TV pitch man, and accused murderer look guilty, or at least menacing. Although art

> Will media consumers come to view journalistic images as nothing more than illustrations? I'd say readers already essentially feel that way. Many magazine editors now use photography simply as illustration for text and not as information in itself. Mistakes like the O.J. cover [on Time] and the retouched teeth of the septuplets' mother [on a Newsweek cover] added to public belief that news organizations will do anything to get bigger audiences, but I think the credibility gap is due to other factors as well, such as the kind of information that gets into print. More and more often it's entertainment news and consumer news, and entertainment imagery is now largely controlled by Hollywood publicists, not editors, so we often see bland illustration rather than brilliant photojournalism.
> — David Schonauer, American Photo[12]

director Arthur Hochstein defended his staff against charges of racism,[13] *Time*'s managing editor admitted he had "never been so wrong about how [a cover] would be received."[14] In a *Cincinnati Enquirer* cartoon, reprinted in *Newsweek*, July 4, 1994, p. 21, *Newsweek*'s relatively unmanipulated O.J. Simpson cover was described as "Real," *Time*'s drastically manipulated cover as "Altered." (The fictitious *Journalism Today* pictured *Homer* Simpson and was labeled "Really Altered.")

Matt Mahurin created the O.J. Simpson photo-illustration and other compelling images in *Time, Life*, and elsewhere. When asked about his inspiration for the Simpson illustration, he said, "He was already a convicted wife-beater. I felt it was a dark moment, whether literally or emotionally, and I made the choice to show that. I truly and honestly thought it was the most innocuous cover I would ever do."[15]

National Geographic's Relocated Pyramids

During the processing of *National Geographic*'s February 1982 photo of the Great Pyramids of Giza, a pyramid was digitally shifted to make the image fit the cover. The alteration provoked much controversy, not so much because it was drastic (it was relatively inconsequential) but because it appeared in a magazine long revered for its authenticity.

In 1998 *National Geographic* editor Bill Allen said,

> Nearly two decades ago we moved one pyramid to get the same effect as if the photographer had walked perhaps fifty yards to the left before taking the photograph. And yet after all that time, one of the most common questions I'm asked is, do you guys still move pyramids? This reminds all of us just how fragile our credibility is. If you lose it, it's almost impossible to ever get

it back. It's why we're such fanatics about disclosure now at *National Geographic*.[16]

(*Note: National Geographic*'s updated, comprehensive policy toward altered photos is in keeping with its hard-won reputation for the highest standards in journalism and wildlife photography.)

IMPROVING UPON NATURE?

Kenneth Brower's article in the May 1998 *Atlantic Monthly*[17] listed a number of staged or otherwise faked nature photos and sequences, including the following:

- a *Life* magazine cover picturing a leopard and its kill in a tree (the leopard was a captive, the antelope was killed by humans, the set-up was shot in different locations over a period of weeks)
- Disney's *The Living Desert* movie (much of which was filmed on fake dunes inside a sound stage)
- a Disney documentary in which a presumably wild hawk intercepts a flying squirrel in mid-air (the hawk had been trained; someone atop a ladder threw dead squirrels at the bird, which missed dozens of times before finally doing its job)
- a view of a polar bear in Antarctica that appeared in a full-page ad for *National Geographic Online* (there are no polar bears in Antarctica; there are polar bears in the Arctic—and also in the Ohio zoo where this particular animal was photographed)[18]

Brower cited a photographer, Tom Mangelson, who had considered the consequences of digital tampering and of shooting "wildlife" photos in commercial game farms and concluded that photographers' incentive to compete in the wild, a sense of adventure, pride in one's work, and public respect for nature photography had all been lost.

Some photographers, concerned that people will assume their photos are fake, have taken to informing viewers that such is not the case. Pacific Northwesterner Lee Mann, for example, includes the following note on his postcards: "None of my cards have been digitally altered." On his web site, he adds: "There are no zoo, game park, aquarium or captive animal photographs in my collection. Also there are no computer-combined photographs."

> Much of the public makes the assumption that photographs appearing in the newspaper are fabricated.
> — Larry Coyne, <u>The Commercial Appeal</u>[19]

OTHER EXAMPLES IN NEWS, SPORTS, ENTERTAINMENT, AND MORE

The following are just some of the many other examples of photomanipulation that have appeared in print.

- The September 8, 2000, edition of the *New York Daily News* carried a picture of President Clinton shaking hands with Fidel Castro.

FIGURES 4.2 and 4.3. The McCaughey septuplets' parents appeared on the covers of both <u>Newsweek</u> and <u>Time</u>. On the former, Mrs. McCaughey's teeth were "fixed" in the photo lab, raising questions about where lines should be drawn when processing images in news publications.

In fact, the handshake was not photographed. The picture was a computerized composite labeled "photo illustration." The paper later admitted that the caption "should have directly said that the image was not an actual photograph."[20]

- The McCaughey septuplets' parents appeared on *Newsweek*'s December 1, 1997, cover (compare Figures 4.2 and 4.3). Mrs. McCaughey's teeth were straightened and whitened by photo technicians, with no mention of the manipulation. In the following issue, the editors explained, "While we often correct color values and contrast levels . . . it is not *Newsweek*'s policy to change or misrepresent the subject matter in any way. We regret the error."

- The winner of a spelling bee sponsored by *The New York Daily News* was photographed for a story in the *New York Post*, whose retouchers removed the name of its rival newspaper from the image of the winner's identification card.[21]
- Gap-toothed Steve Yzerman was captain of the Red Wings when they won the Stanley Cup in 1997. *The Detroit News* commissioned Triumph Books of Chicago to produce a special commemorative volume. Yzerman appeared on its cover sporting a new tooth, courtesy of Triumph's digital orthodontists. The paper's director of photography said, "We were as outraged as the rest of the journalism community . . . neither I nor anyone else in the photo department knew about [the alteration] until we saw the book in print."[22] Later printings featured the unaltered version.
- By the time Cher's photo appeared on the cover of the November 1996 *Ladies' Home Journal*, her tattoo had been removed and her dress replaced. The singer/actress also claimed that her torso had been replaced with that of a model, although the magazine denied it.[23]
- John Filo won a Pulitzer Prize for a photo taken on May 4, 1970, at an antiwar protest at Kent State University. National Guard riflemen had killed four students and wounded several others. In the photo, Mary Ann Vecchio cries out and gestures as she kneels over the body of student Jeffrey Miller. A fence post behind Ms. Vecchio's head was removed from a reprint appearing in the May 1995 issue of *Life* magazine, sparking heated debate. Said *Life*'s director of photography David Friend, "*Life* did not and does not manipulate news photos. The photo we published was supplied to us by our photo library . . . Amazingly, the fence post had been airbrushed out by someone, now anonymous, in a darkroom sometime in the early 1970s."
- *Newsweek* added supermarket bar codes to the nose cones of fighter jets in a 1991 cover photo for a story titled "Arms for Sale" (Figure 4.4). While it could be argued that the alteration was obvious and therefore likely to mislead no one, manipulating a photograph in a news context where unmanipulated photography is the norm may be an example of the most troubling use of the new technology.
- The cover of *Rodale's Scuba Diving* magazine's October 1994 issue showed a diver in exciting proximity to a sting ray; in fact, the ray was "imported" from a different photo. There was no disclosure of the composite in that issue.
- Olympic rivals Nancy Kerrigan and Tonya Harding seemed to skate side by side in a composite photo on the front page of *New York Newsday* before they actually set foot on the ice of Lillehammer.[24] See Chapter 16.
- One person was deleted from the center of a news photo appearing in the *Asbury Park Press*, New Jersey's third largest newspaper. The space was filled with cloned portions of a background object.[25]

FIGURE 4.4.   Bar codes on jet fighters? Some people believed that the implausibility of the image excused the manipulation, but others were troubled by the use of such techniques on the cover of a news magazine.

- In all of their outdoor photos of the 1984 Summer Olympic Games, editors at the *Orange County Register* changed the color of the metropolitan Los Angeles sky (notorious for its smog) to clear blue.[26]
- As a practical joke, a lab technician at the Gainesville (Florida) *Sun* digitally altered a license plate hanging on the wall in a photograph; "SEMINOLES" became "SEMIHOLES." "Seminoles" is the nickname of Florida State University students and athletic teams. Gainesville is the home of rival University of Florida. The technician, a student at the University of Florida, resigned.[27]

- Actress Mary Martin was digitally removed when *The Washington Post* in 1993 republished a 1987 photograph of actress Helen Hayes standing in front of Martin. *The Washington Post* has a policy against changing news photographs, but as the *Post*'s assistant managing editor for photography admitted, "we did end up altering reality."[28]
- Bitter Texas political rivals Clayton Williams and Ann Richards seemed to embrace each other in a photo on *Texas Monthly*'s October 1990 "Dirty Dancing" cover; in fact, the image was a composite with transplanted heads.
- A *Texas Monthly* cover featured a head-transplant composite of retiring governor Ann Richards clad in leather and sitting on a motorcycle. An AP wire story mentioned the governor's motorcycle riding; it used the cover as an illustration but did not mention that the photo was a fake, compounding its potential for misleading readers.[29]
- On a 1989 *TV Guide* cover, Oprah Winfrey's head was placed atop the body of Ann-Margret (actually, the torso was a drawing based on a photo of Ann-Margret).[30]
- Dustin Hoffman and Tom Cruise appeared side by side in *Newsweek* but not in real life, *Newsweek* (Jan. 16, 1989);[31] see (Figure 4.5).

Some professionals might consider a few of this chapter's examples to be relatively innocuous, but in most of the cases readers were left in the dark. We can identify these images as ones in which nonfiction photography's

FIGURE 4.5. Do "photo ops" entail standards less rigorous than "hard news"? Dustin Hoffman and Tom Cruise appear to be enjoying each other's company, but this is a composite of photos taken at different places and times.

presumed relationship to reality was disrupted, although readers might have a simpler description. They might call them lies.

One profound result of all this was expressed by *Texas Monthly* art director D.J. Stout: "Altered photographs were really hurting the integrity of the magazine's cover, to the point that when we had a great photograph, nobody believed it."[32] This loss of faith was reflected in the July/August 1995 issue of *American Photo*, which reported the results of a readers poll. To the question "Do you think that the credibility of journalism is in jeopardy because of digital photographic technology?" 88 respondents said yes, 11 said no, and 4 said "not sure."[33]

SUBVERTED CERTAINTIES

As author and professor William J. Mitchell wrote, "[Photographs] were generally regarded as causally generated, truthful reports about things in the real world, unlike more traditionally handcrafted images, which seemed notoriously ambiguous and uncertain human constructions. The emergence of digital imaging has irrevocably subverted these certainties, forcing us to adopt a far more wary and vigilant interpretive stance."[34] Dino Brugioni is the author of *Photo Fakery: The History and Techniques of Photographic Deception and Manipulation*. He has said, "Photography shouldn't be accepted as prima facie evidence in court any longer—digital cameras can erase the evidence."[35] The *Sacramento Bee*'s J.D. Lasica went so far as to conclude, "the 1980s may be the last decade in which photos could be considered evidence of anything."[36]

Will Andy Grunberg's sobering prediction at the beginning of this chapter come to pass? Will media consumers come to view journalistic images as nothing more than illustrations, like drawings or cartoons? If they do, what will have been lost? Would such a sea change affect our faith in media, government, and other public and private institutions? We would do well to consider the implications not only in terms of everyday journalistic practice but also in terms of how we perceive ourselves and our relationships to our fellow citizens, our communities, our world.

SUMMARY

The inherent trustworthiness once attributed to photography is withering, at least in the opinion of many observers. Whether it will vanish altogether is an open question. In any case, from now on, assumptions once taken for granted will be scrutinized with suspicion—for good reason. Visual journalists will have to accommodate these shifts and re-examine their own practices and obligations of disclosure if they are to successfully separate their work from art, cartoons, fantasy, and fiction. These issues, and some others raised by the examples in this chapter, are addressed later in our discussion.

EXPLORATIONS

1. What would be your answer to the question posed by *American Photo*'s poll: Is the credibility of journalism in jeopardy because of digital photography?

2. Regarding *Newsweek*'s bar-coded fighter jets (Figure 4.4): While it could be argued that the alteration was so obvious that few readers could be misled, critics might assert that the cover of a leading news magazine is one of the last places one would expect to find an altered photo, and therefore the danger of misleading the public is substantial. What do you think? Would the photo have been more or less ethical in a different context?

    What if the photo had been further altered to make it look *less* real? Suppose, for example, the bar-coded jets were stacked up in a fictional supermarket setting, along with bar-coded canned goods and TV dinners, such that no reader would have mistaken the image for a "real" photo. Would it have been any more or less ethical? Why?

3. Regarding the composite photo of Tom Cruise and Dustin Hoffman (Figure 4.5), what does its appearance in *Newsweek* mean in terms of its reality or ethics? What sorts of expectations do readers bring to the pages of national news magazines? Would the undisclosed composite be any more or less ethical if the image had appeared in a daily newspaper? In a glossy magazine devoted to covering celebrities? Why or why not?

    In general, would you apply the same ethical standards to (a) a daily newspaper such as the *Chicago Tribune*; (b) a weekly news magazine such as *Time*; and (c) a more or less general interest consumer magazine such as *GQ* or *Details*? What differences might we expect, if any, in the assumptions typical readers bring to photos appearing in these types of publications? Would such differences, if any, affect the ethics of photo manipulation?

ENDNOTES

1. Andy Grunberg, "Ask It No Questions: The Camera Can Lie," *The New York Times* (August 12, 1990): Sec. 2, p. 1.
2. One effect facilitated by the new technology might be called reverse cropping: It's easy to use cloning and brush tools to extend a photo's borders.
3. The technology is so pervasive that the magazine *Photo Electronic Imaging* is devoted exclusively to "integrating photography, electronic imaging, and graphics." Other examples: *Digital Imaging* and *Digital Photo World* magazines.
4. David Schonauer, "The Future of Photography 1997," *American Photo* (November/December 1997): 47.
5. From an e-mail correspondence with the author, fall 1998.
6. On that same program, a reporter elaborated on long-accepted practices: "Hues, tones, and contrast have always been determined in the darkroom after the picture was snapped, but now, whoever controls the mouse can change nearly everything about an image."

7. J.D. Lasica, "Photographs That Lie: The Ethical Dilemma of Digital Retouching," *Washington Journalism Review* (June 1989): 23.

8. "Kennedy: The Torch Passes," *Spy* (November 1993); Letters (February 1994): 8. The practice of putting a famous person's head on another's body became common in the early 1990s; such images are now known in some industry circles as "zipper heads." See Jonathan Alter, "When Photographs Lie," *Newsweek* (July 30, 1990): 45.

9. Stephanie Dolgoff, "The Real India: Fantasy, Not Fakery," *American Photo* (November/December 1993): 28.

10. Monitor column, "The Color of Mommy: Lanting's Chick Scene," *American Photo* (July/August 1996): 32.

11. See Joseph P. Kahn, "When 1 Picture Tells 2 Stories," *The Boston Globe* (June 22, 1994): Living, 21; Howard Kurtz, "*Time* to *Newsweek*: What's Wrong with This Picture?" *The Washington Post* (June 24, 1994): Style, B1; Rita Ciolli, "*Time* Alters Photograph for Its Cover," *Newsday* (June 22, 1994): 25; "Photo Flap: *Time*'s Altered Image Sparks Ethics Debate," *The Phoenix Gazette* (June 22, 1994): A2; Howard Kurtz, "*Time*'s 'Sinister' Simpson; Cover Photo Was Computer-Enhanced," *The Washington Post* (June 22, 1994): Style, D1.

12. David Schonauer is the editor in chief of *American Photo*. From an e-mail correspondence with the author, fall 1998.

13. He said, "These sinister motives that were attributed to us were just not true. Had the people saying that done a little basic reporting by asking me about it directly, they would have found that out. What we found out was that it's very easy to inadvertently fan the flames on a very hot topic." *Print* (March/April 1996): 21.

14. James R. Gaines, "To Our Readers," *Time* (July 4, 1994): 4. The managing editor cited the charge by the NAACP's Benjamin Chavis that it portrayed Simpson as "some kind of animal." According to Joseph P. Kahn, it was "as if Willie Horton had stepped out of an old Republican campaign ad and into O.J.'s cleats." Kahn, 21.

15. Janet Abrams, "Little Photoshop of Horrors: The Ethics of Manipulating Journalistic Imagery," *Print* (November/December 1995): 33.

16. From an e-mail correspondence with the author, fall 1998.

17. Kenneth Brower, "Photography in the Age of Falsification," *Atlantic Monthly* (May 1998): 92–111.

18. *National Geographic* front-of-book section, September 1996.

19. Larry Coyne is the director of photography at *The Commercial Appeal*. Larry Coyne, "Visual Credibility as Important as Honest Reporting," *Viewpoint*, Scripps Howard News (July/August 1995): 24.

20. *New York Daily News* (September 11, 2001): News and Views/City Beat.

21. Wendy Bounds, "How Should You Spell Archrival? In New York, It's D-a-i-l-y N-e-w-s," *Wall Street Journal* (June 2, 1997): B1.

22. Jim Gordon, "Oops! Again over Covers," *News Photographer* (September 1997): 6.

23. Jean Seligmann, "Cher Gets an Unwanted Makeover," *Newsweek* (October 21, 1996): 95.

24. "Fire on Ice," *Newsday* (Feb. 16, 1994): 1; see Chapter 16; see also William Glaberson, "*Newsday* Imagines an Event, and Sets Off a Debate," *The New York Times* (February 17, 1994): A12.

25. Lasica, 22.

26. Lasica, 22.

27. Julie Babcock, "Altered Photo Brings Lab Tech's Resignation," *News Photographer* (March 1994): 11.

28. Suzan Revah, "Mary Martin Has Left the Building," *American Journalism Review* (May 1993): 13.

29. The cover story was "White Hot Mama," *Texas Monthly* (July 1994). Chip Brown (AP), "Texas Governor Will Be Missed by Friends and Foes," *The Bulletin*, Bend, Oregon (November 11, 1994): A4.

30. See Jacques Leslie, "Digital Photopros and Photo(shop) Realism," *Wired* (May 1995): 108–13; see also J.D. Reed, "Return of the Body Snatcher," *Time* (September 4, 1989): 4; Patty Rhule, "TV Guide Snatches a Body," *USA Today* (August 29, 1989): 1.

31. See Shiela Reaves, "What's Wrong with This Picture? Attitudes of Photographic Editors at Daily Newspapers and Their Tolerance toward Digital Manipulation," a paper presented at the annual convention of the Association for Education in Journalism and Mass Communication (AEJMC), Boston, August 1991: 147; C. Ansberry, "Alterations of Photos Raises Host of Legal, Ethical Issues," *The Wall Street Journal* (January 26, 1989): Sec. 2, p. 1.

32. Leslie, 113.

33. Carol Squiers, "The AP Poll: Should Altered Images Be Marked? Our Readers Tell Us What They Think," *American Photo* (July/August 1995): 96. On the other hand, the cover story of the September/October 1996 issue ("Is Photojournalism Dead?") cited the proliferation of digital

media as one reason for "doomful predictions" but concentrated more on other factors such as the public's apparent preference for celebrity photography and the decline of magazines such as the old *Life*. The article asserted, "You'd never suspect the growing threat of new technology when you see the quantity, and quality, of still pictures being made by photojournalists today." Carol Squiers, "The Truth of Our Time: The Death and Continuing Life of Photojournalism," *American Photo* (September/October 1996): 56.

34. William J. Mitchell, "When Is Seeing Believing? Digital Technology for Manipulating Images Has Subverted the Certainty of Photographic Evidence," *Scientific American* (February 1994): 73.

35. Andrew Curry, "Now You See Him, Now You Don't," *U.S. News & World Report* (July 9–16, 2001): 46.

36. Lasica, 25.

Chapter 5

Rationales and Excuses

Justifying Staged and Manipulated Photos

Many people do not see any difference [between] covering a subject and asking the people involved to do something for our cameras because that is what they do—they just don't happen to be doing it at the moment. The difference is being committed to the documentary photograph, therefore assuring our readers that the pictures are accurate . . . and our visual reporting is just that—reporting.

—Larry Coyne, *The Commercial Appeal*[1]

IN DEFENSE

The previous chapter cited two notorious examples of altered photography, among others: *Time* magazine's 1994 cover photo of O.J. Simpson, and *National Geographic*'s 1982 cover featuring a relocated pyramid. This chapter reveals what professionals at those two magazines had to say in defense of their actions and then explores other proposed justifications for altered photography in mass media.

NOT THAT BIG A DEAL

Some explanations downplay the significance of the alterations, perhaps assuming readers' awareness of photo manipulation or their indifference to it.

Mona Lisa with a Graffiti Mustache

In defense of *Time*'s alteration of the O.J. Simpson mug shot, art director Arthur Hochstein said, "We knew [the original photo] would be widely disseminated, and that gave us license, we felt, to push the image into something more interpretive or illustrative."[2] This seems to invoke the "Mona Lisa with a graffiti mustache" rationale: The original is already familiar to the public; therefore, our alteration will be instantly recognizable and readers will not be misled.

> It's getting to the point where newspapers and magazines are in the same boat as any other commodity. They are products that consumers have to be convinced to buy. Pressures come down from the top because shareholders need to be satisfied. It really shouldn't be a surprise if more illustration is done because it is a manifestation of the bright, garish MTV-like society in which we live. With that said, I firmly believe there will always be people who want and expect quality and honesty in the publications they read, people who want to see the reality or actuality of a situation, scene, or moment in time.
> —Les Riess, American Society of Media Photographers[3]

We can imagine cases when this argument might indeed help justify an altered image (imagine a "photo" in which the Statue of Liberty wears gigantic sunglasses and holds a surfboard). But *Time*'s altered image appeared only days after the public's exposure to the original mug shot, which had scant opportunity to acquire icon status. Furthermore, the alterations were not obvious enough to be grasped by many viewers, at least at first glance.

Could Have Moved the Camera

After *National Geographic* shifted a pyramid in the "digital darkroom," its director of photography explained that the photographer could have moved the camera at the scene to get the same result.[4] A *National Geographic* editor maintained that cropping is a more serious alteration.[5]

No One Believes It Anyway

Occasionally a heavily manipulated photo appears in *National Enquirer* or a similar tabloid. Some argue that such publications are known for sensational or even ludicrous stories and have little credibility to begin with, so their photo alterations are not significant. Critics of this defense might point out that in recent years *National Enquirer* has made efforts to increase its credibility.

IN CONSIDERATION OF OUR READERS

Some rationales cite the readers' best interests—the photo was risqué, politically incorrect, or otherwise offensive.

A Matter of Taste

Super model Kate Moss was pictured in a tight-fitting gauzy top on the cover of *American Photo* (Figure 5.1). The editors digitally removed her

FIGURE 5.1.   When Kate Moss appeared on the cover of <u>American Photo</u>, her nipples were removed as "a matter of taste." An apparently unmanipulated version of the same photo appeared inside.

nipples as "a matter of taste." There was no disclosure of the cover alteration in the issue (January/February 1994), although it was subsequently disclosed in response to a letter to the editor.[6]

Cosmopolitan magazine illustrated a travel piece with Ruth Orkin's famous 1951 photo, "American Girl in Italy," in which a strolling young woman has drawn the attention of several rowdy locals. When it was reprinted a decade later in the *Life World Library,* an onlooker who appeared to be holding his crotch was airbrushed from the image.[7]

A color photo appearing in a newspaper pictured a young boy; a barely noticeable detail was that the zipper on his pants was open. The published version was altered to close the zipper.[8]

> Photography will continue to be a democratized medium that can take us anywhere and flesh out the graphic reality that words could never express. No matter that photographs are only <u>images</u> of reality or that photographs no longer are accepted in Canadian courtrooms as evidence, we still believe them and I still believe in the credibility of photography. Perhaps Lewis Hine summed it up best: "If I could tell the story in words, I wouldn't have to lug a camera." Amen.
>
> —Bill Ryan, University of Oregon[9]

When a towel worn by an otherwise unclothed athlete left him partially exposed, *National Geographic* digitally extended the garment.[10]

Popular Photography's publishing director recalled that at one newspaper he had worked for, no photo of a male dog could be published unless the animal's genitals had been removed from the photo with an airbrush.[11]

In 1996 the Louisville *Courier-Journal* ran a photo of a stripper executing a high kick before patrons at a bar. The woman did not appear to be wearing underwear. Instead of running a less compelling image (or no image), editors reluctantly "fixed" the photo on a computer by extending the dancer's clothing.[12]

Too Shocking

Wanting to provide realistic accounts of crimes, battles, and natural disasters and yet not wanting to offend readers, editors have long debated the appropriateness of showing photos of dead bodies. After the August 1998 U.S. embassy bombing in Kenya, *The Los Angeles Times* ran a photo of a Nairobi morgue that depicted several corpses. *The New York Times* used the same photo but cropped out the bodies. *The San Francisco Examiner* ran the photo full-frame, but intentionally blurred the image of a charred corpse; *Examiner* editors later said they should not have done so.[13]

Political Correctness

In the fall of 2000, The University of Wisconsin manipulated the cover of a brochure by inserting the image of a black student into a crowd of white football fans, so as to suggest racial diversity in the student body. The University's publications director admitted the move was "an error in judgment."

A print advertisement for a brewer pictured a large group of people, ostensibly employees, photographed from above; the crowd was in the shape of a U.S. map. After the company's minority hiring practices were publicly assailed, the ad was altered so that many white faces were replaced with nonwhites.[14]

Media critics and old-fashioned photographers may lament loose modern visual standards and the unrepentant use of digital hocus-pocus in a wide variety of editorial imagery, but popular taste, trained by a polysaturated diet of action movies and MTV, demands ever greater visual pyrotechnics.

—David Schonauer, American Photo[15]

Before publishing three photos of baseball caps, the *Seattle Times* deleted the Cleveland Indians' mascot, "Chief Wahoo," a grinning carica-ture of a Native American considered by many to be offensive. In admitting that the alteration was an error, Managing Editor Alex MacLeod explained, "The photo manipulation was well intentioned, but the result was a visual lie."[16]

James Dean was a rebel without a smoke when the *Deseret News* of Salt Lake City digitally erased the film icon's near-trademark cigarette from a photo in one of its summer 2001 editions. The newspaper is owned by the Church of Jesus Christ of Latter-day Saints, and most of its 66,000 sub-scribers are church members, who avoid the consumption of tobacco in any form. The manipulation violated the paper's policy but was effected anyway when staffers were unable to locate a cigarette-free photo before deadline.

Finally, Mississippi Delta singer/guitarist Robert Johnson was immor-talized on a U.S. postage stamp whose design was based on a photo. The legendary bluesman's cigarette was removed from the image (one of very few authentic photos of Johnson known to exist) because an advisory citi-zens' group "didn't want the stamps to be perceived as promoting ciga-rettes," according to a Post Office spokeswoman.[17]

WE PLAY BY DIFFERENT RULES

Some nonfiction editors and their associates believe that their publications (or certain aspects of them) hold a special status that allows extra leeway in processing images.

House and Garden, Fact and Fantasy

In some "shelter" magazines, as they are called, photos of homes and gar-dens are substantially altered. After estimating that 45 of his 48 magazine covers had been digitally manipulated, an art director told Professor Shiela Reaves that magazines such as *HG* and *Better Homes & Gardens* are "deal-ing in dreams"; they are "motivators" and "idea generators." He added, "They are not reportage even though we shoot people's homes."[18]

Covers Are Different

On the cover of the book *A Day In The Life of America: Photographed by 200 of the World's Leading Photojournalists on One Day,* the image of the moon was enlarged and the horizontal photo was made vertical by moving

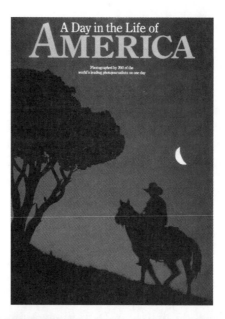

FIGURE 5.2. Some people believe that book covers are "advertising" and thus entail non-photojournalistic standards. Still, along with featuring a substantially manipulated image (top), this cover promises that the book contains the work of photojournalists. The original photo (bottom) was taken by Frans Lanting, who says, "I insist on an accurate portrayal of events; the altered version was published without my knowledge or permission."

the silhouettes of a horseman, a hill, and a tree (Figure 5.2).[19] The photo director argued that it was permissible to manipulate the images because covers are "advertising"—their primary function is to sell the book.[20]

CLOSE ENOUGH TO REALITY

Some justifications for manipulating images call into question the relationship between a nonfiction photo and the reality it purportedly reflects.

It Happened

One rationalization boils down to this: It happened. This argument allows that while faking a photo to mislead readers may be unethical, faking a photo to *inform* readers is acceptable; a staged, doctored, or otherwise phony photo is ethical if it portrays an event that actually happened.

One example of the "it happened" rationale occurred in the summer of 1925, when the *New York News* sent a photographer to get a picture of a cat carrying her kitten across a busy street and tying up traffic. By the time the photographer arrived, the event had passed, so he set up the shot, putting the cats back across the street (twice) until he got the picture he wanted.

It Could Have Happened

A close relative of "it happened" is the "it *could* have happened" rationale. The previous chapter cited a cover of *Rodale's Scuba Diving* magazine in which a sting ray had been "imported" from another photo (Figure 5.3). One reader recognized the manipulation and wrote in to complain, saying, "There's nothing wrong with that, so long as it's stated in the photo credit. But to pass this off as just another outstanding cover shot is misleading." The photographer responded: "The sting ray was added not to fool people, but as a creative device to make the cover design more appealing. Since [*Rodale's Scuba Diving*] is not a journal of natural history, I think photographic illustrations can be modified to some extent without additional caption—so long as the illustration remains plausible. As this one is."[21]

The "it could have happened" rationale was called into question when *Los Angeles Times* photographer Mike Meadows was suspended without pay and moved to an administrative position after it was alleged he had staged a photograph of a firefighter cooling off with water from a swimming pool during the Fall 1993 fires in Southern California (Figure 5.4).[22] Meadows emphatically denied that he had posed or staged the photo, but the controversy raised a provocative question: Suppose a photographer *does* pose a photo of a scene or event which he or she has witnessed. Writing in *The New Republic*, Michael Lewis asserted that even if the allegations against Meadows had been proved, "[The firefighter photo] is especially interesting because its fiction is so harmless. . . . The image is perfectly true to the event in most of what it conveys, to wit: (a) that fighting fires makes

FIGURE 5.3. Do readers expect magazine covers like this one to portray real people and actual events? In this composite, photos of the diver and the sting ray were taken at different places, different times.

you hot, (b) that houses of people rich enough to own swimming pools also burn to the ground, (c) that even firemen realize that it's pointless to fight a house fire when there's nothing left of the house, and (d) that there is a certain irony in running out of water pressure—as the fireman had—when you are standing beside a giant swimming pool. The photograph challenges a crucial news-gathering conceit: that respectable journalism is a passive exercise in fact-gathering that conveys to the reader an unadulterated slice of reality. This piece of propaganda is a far greater threat to the truth than anything in the photograph."[23]

FIGURE 5.4. When this photo was published, some people questioned whether it was staged. Photographer Mike Meadows told the author, "I shoot breaking news, period. I would never stage a photo." Some people defended it either way, including a writer who claimed in The New Republic that the notion of photographic objectivity is "a far greater threat to the truth than anything in [this] photograph."

SUMMARY

Professional journalists have altered mass-media photos for reasons of taste or political correctness; because they believed the alterations to be so obvious as to be instantly recognizable or so minor as to be ethically insignificant; or because the results could have been accomplished by other, acceptable, methods. Some journalists have subdivided their work into categories with different standards of processing or disclosure. Others have adopted the curious rationalization that it is appropriate to illustrate nonfiction text with unlabeled fiction, or the assumption that journalism includes accounts not only of events that occurred but also events that *could* have occurred.

If these rationalizations were ludicrous or sleazy, it would be easy to write them off to low ethical standards. But most were offered by responsible professionals acting in good faith. In some cases, the manipulations sparked public complaints that resulted in apologies and stricter codes. In others, though, publishers continued to defend their manipulations as reasonable and ethical. These discussions still frame the debate.

In review, Part I of this book explained that faith in photographic authenticity has been rooted in the manner in which photos seem to reflect objective reality. That faith also depends on assumptions that faked or manipulated mass-media photos are exceptions, to be considered "staged" or "doctored." Part II examined digital media's signal characteristic, its malleability. It also revealed technology's new threat to photocredibility, and listed examples of manipulated images in news, sports, entertainment, and other fields, as well as presenting rationalizations offered in their defense.

One purpose of this book is to suggest guidelines that will enable visual journalists in all media to creatively explore digital technology while preserving their credibility. Before looking ahead, Part III looks back to the philosophical underpinnings of journalistic ethics, as well as the traditions and conventions of photojournalism. After all, photographers have wrestled with the ethics of published imagery since the dawn of photography in the mid-19th century.

EXPLORATIONS

1. Re-examine *Time*'s rationale for its O.J. Simpson cover—that readers, already familiar with the original mug shot, would recognize the altered version as either visual commentary or artistic statement. Is the argument convincing? How recognizable must an image be in order for its adaptation or parody to be immediately grasped by typical viewers? Might narrowly targeted audiences be more likely to recognize certain images? Can you think of famous images that are often parodied or appropriated for journalistic or advertising purposes?

2. Shelter magazines have long engaged in "propping"—adding furniture, flowers, framed paintings, and so on to homes before photographing them, sometimes even replacing most or all of the residents' own possessions with objects borrowed from galleries and furniture stores. Recall the art director's claim that house and garden magazines are "dealing in dreams" and "are not reportage even though we shoot people's homes." Do you agree? When viewing photos of homes and gardens in magazines devoted to decorating, landscaping, and architecture, do readers expect fictional "dreams" instead of real photos? Or are readers'

expectations and values simply incompatible with the commercial aspirations or aesthetic tastes of some editors and art directors?

3. Regarding the altered photo of Kate Moss on the cover of *American Photo*, one could argue that while subscription copies go only to readers who ask for and expect the publication, newsstand or store-rack copies are on public display, seen by passersby who happen to look in their direction; therefore, it is permissible to alter cover photos if they might offend some casual viewers. What do you think?

4. Regarding the uncredited composite photo on the cover of a scuba magazine, do you accept the photographer's "it could have happened" rationale? Or do consumers of magazines devoted to underwater pursuits (or motorcycle racing, mountain climbing, or any outdoor, sporting, or travel topics) expect the photos to reflect actual scenes and activities?

5. Reconsider the "no one believes it anyway" rationale. Even if we accept that the *National Enquirer* and similar publications may not have the reputation of *The Wall Street Journal*, what about their impact on passersby who absorb, consciously or subconsciously, their covers' prominent elements without seeing disclaimers, or without considering the publication's reputation, or without even noticing its name?

6. Reconsider the controversial photo of the firefighter. As noted, the photographer explained that he did *not* stage it after all. Some people defended it either way. For example, Michael Lewis suggested that even if it had been staged, as alleged, any shortcomings of a posed photo of an event that actually occurred are insignificant compared to the bigger conceits of "objective" reporting. Do you agree? What is the implication of authenticity of a newspaper photo that accompanies a news article? Does it mean: Here is something that happened; we caught it on film? Or is it close enough if a news photo, without disclosure of the posing, portrays a staged event, something realistic-looking, something that *could* have happened?

ENDNOTES

1. Larry Coyne, "Visual Credibility as Important as Honest Reporting," *Viewpoint*, Scripps Howard News (July/August 1995): 24.
2. Joseph P. Kahn, "When 1 Picture Tells 2 Stories," *The Boston Globe* (June 22, 1994): Living, 21.
3. Mr. Riess is the president and chairman of the Board of ASMP. From an e-mail correspondence with the author, fall 1998.
4. *1987 Associated Press Managing Editors Photo & Graphics Report*: 10. The editor in chief, Bill Garrett, was also quoted in T. Druckrey, "From Reproduction to Technology," *Afterimage* (November 1989): 12–13.
5. "Retouching Poses Ethical Questions," *Folio:* (March 1985): 19–20.
6. A small, apparently unmanipulated version of the photo appeared on the contents page. The disclosure appeared in Letters, *American Photo* (March/April 1994): 13.
7. Janet Abrams, "Little Photoshop of Horrors: The Ethics of Manipulating Journalistic Imagery," *Print* (November/December 1995): 45.

8. In a survey of photo editors, 71% disagreed with the alteration. Shiela Reaves, "What's Wrong with This Picture?: Daily Newspaper Photo Editors' Attitudes and Their Tolerance toward Digital Manipulation," *Newspaper Research Journal* (fall 1992/winter 1993): 131–55.

9. From an e-mail correspondence with the author, fall 1998.

10. Tony Kelly, "Manipulating Reality: Digital Alteration of Photos Discussed at Poynter Seminar," *Editor & Publisher* (June 8, 1991): 16.

11. Arthur Goldsmith, "Photos Always Lied," *Popular Photography* (November 1991): 68.

12. Wilson Lowrey, "Altered Plates: Photo Manipulation and the Search for News Value in the 1920s and 1990s," a paper presented to the annual convention of the Association for Education in Journalism and Mass Communication (AEJMC), Visual Communication Division, Baltimore, MD, August 1998.

13. Felicity Barringer, "Breaking a Taboo, Editors Turn to Images of Death," *The New York Times* (October 25, 1998): Section 4, p. 1.

14. "Visual Enhancement of Photos," *Editor & Publisher* (March 25, 1989): 46. In an odd reversal of that same idea, the Ford Motor Company effectively removed black and Indian workers from an advertising brochure by digitally lightening their skin color, changing their hairstyles, and removing clothing deemed excessively "ethnic." Edgar Shaohua Huang, "Readers' Perception of Digital Alteration and Truth-Value in Documentary Photographs," submitted in partial fulfillment for a Ph.D. degree, School of Journalism, Indiana University (October 1999): 12.

15. David Schonauer, "In Camera" column, *American Photo* (July/August 1999): 33.

16. *Associated Press,* March 31, 1997.

17. *Associated Press,* September 17, 1994, *Register-Guard,* Eugene, OR, 13A.

18. Shiela Reaves, "Digital Alteration of Photographs in Magazines: An Examination of the Ethics," a paper presented to the annual convention of the AEJMC, Washington, D.C., August, 1989: 10.

19. According to Paul Lester, other members of the *A Day in the Life* series—books on Australia, Canada, and California—all featured altered covers. Paul Lester, *Photojournalism: An Ethical Approach* (Hillsdale, NJ: Lawrence Erlbaum Assoc., 1991), 124.

20. "When Seeing Isn't Believing," *Life* Special Anniversary Issue (Fall 1988): 160.

21. Letters, *Rodale's Scuba Diving* (March 1995): 6.

22. Photographer Mike Meadows had worked at the *Times* since 1961. Michael Lewis, "Lights! Camera! News!," *The New Republic* (February 28, 1994): 11.

23. Lewis: 11.

III

Groundwork: Toward a Protocol

Chapter 6

Ethical Foundations
Doing the Right Thing

The only way in which a human being can make some approach to knowing the whole of a subject is by hearing what can be said about it by persons of every variety of opinion, and studying all modes in which it can be looked at by every character of mind. No wise man ever acquired his wisdom in any mode but this.
—John Stuart Mill, *On Liberty*

Suppose you live in an apartment, and your next-door neighbor is blasting his Limp Bizkit CDs at an earsplitting volume well past midnight. After two hours of wrapping a pillow around your head you go next door to complain. Your neighbor's response: "It's a free country. Get lost." He slams the door, leaving you to ponder not only his right to play his compact discs but also your own right to get a good night's sleep.

In solving this conflict, it may seem odd to consult the wisdom of a Greek philosopher who was born more than two thousand years ago, but Aristotle did indeed address the competing interests of individuals, and the balance between the rights of the individual versus those of the community. These issues and many others were also explored in great depth by his teacher, Plato, and by Plato's teacher, Socrates. It is anyone's guess what these titans of the classical age would have made of compact-disc technology (not to mention Limp Bizkit), but their teachings are woven throughout the fabric of Western philosophy, which over the centuries has helped to shape evolving theories of society, codes of conduct, and professional standards, including those of today's visual journalists.

THE BRANCHES OF PHILOSOPHY

To the ancient Greeks, the word "philosophy" meant the love of wisdom. The field is typically divided into five related areas: logic, which formulates laws and procedures pertaining to valid reasoning; aesthetics, which seeks

> When I first put a video camera on my shoulder for an
> upstart news channel called Cable News Network, the ques-
> tion of ethics in photojournalism had never been broached to
> me. There were no college courses devoted to the examination
> and discussion of ethical questions for photographers. There
> were no assignment editors or bureau chiefs who laid down
> the law. . . . There were no hard and fast rules. Basically, it
> seemed as though each photographer lived and worked
> according to his own ethical standards.
>
> —William Langley, videographer[1]

to establish artistic criteria and to reveal the nature of beauty; metaphysics,
which addresses the nature of existence and the ultimate meaning of the uni-
verse; epistemology, which examines the nature of knowledge and methods
of knowing; and ethics.

"ETHICS" DEFINED

The studies of philosophy, religion, and morality have intertwined for
thousands of years, as thinkers have grappled with the deepest questions of
meaning and existence. Why are we here? Are we the masters of our des-
tinies, or are we swept about by capricious winds of fate? Do our lives spin
inexorably toward a predetermined destination like so many gears in some
fixed, cosmic machine, or are they part of a miraculous plan conceived by
an all-knowing god?

Like the study of law, the study of ethics addresses how our answers
to philosophy's profound questions ultimately influence our everyday decision making and how we treat each other in our personal, communal, and
professional lives. Ethics (a word that appears both in singular and plural
constructions) presupposes a human being's awareness of right and wrong,
and evaluates human conduct as reflective of moral values. More specifically, ethics refers to a discipline, theory, or other system that seeks to
provide moral guidelines by integrating or balancing personal values with
institutional or community obligations.

The goal of ethics, then, is to improve society as well as the individual.
In their most concrete expressions, ethical standards are spelled out in codes
and lists of rules. These codes and lists reflect general principles, which in
turn may be rooted in multiple sources such as the teachings of social and
political philosophers, legal documents such as the First Amendment to the
U.S. Constitution, and religious dictates such as the Golden Rule and the
Ten Commandments.

> Now of all things good, truth holds the first place among gods and men alike.
>
> — Plato, <u>Laws, V</u>

The Ninth Commandment

According to the Old Testament's Book of Exodus, Moses descended from Mount Sinai after a conversation with God and delivered to the Israelites two tablets of stone. Upon these tablets were inscribed ten laws forbidding polytheism, idolatry, murder, theft, and other crimes and sins. Of particular interest to journalists is the Ninth Commandment: "Thou shalt not bear false witness against thy neighbor."

In other words: Tell the truth. This simple dictate has for millennia informed the laws and philosophies not only of those who look to the Bible for inspiration but of secular entities as well, such as governments, media organizations, and professional societies.

The Golden Rule

Another familiar Biblical phrase appears in the New Testament's Books of Matthew and Luke as one of the sayings of Jesus of Nazareth: "Do unto others as you would have them do unto you," or "Love thy neighbor as thyself" (the sentiment was expressed by Plato some four centuries earlier). Many authors of ethical codes have invoked this principle in the belief that if every member of society treated every other member with the sensitivity and respect all of us desire, human existence would be characterized by kindness, peace, and tranquillity.

Aristotle's Golden Mean

It is the Greeks of the ancient world to whom we owe the very idea of rational inquiry independent of religious dogma. Aristotle (384–322 B.C.) enrolled in Plato's Academy as a teenager. His curiosity was so broad and his intellectual stamina was so great that he came to be considered the most educated person of his era. In today's terms his accomplishments would have embraced ground-breaking discoveries and entire careers in botany, biology, physics, metaphysics, natural history, ethics, literary criticism, and other fields. His establishment of rational principles formed the basis for scientific procedures that were followed for centuries to come. His theories of logic still stand.

Aristotelian philosophy holds that the goal of life is happiness, to be achieved not by sensual pleasure and wealth but through reflection upon philosophical truth. Of particular interest to our inquiry is Aristotle's Golden Mean, which looks for solutions to ethical dilemmas in the middle

ground between extreme viewpoints. This does not suggest merely wavering
without purpose between conflicting opinions, nor does it entail using some
sort of arithmetic to calculate a precise midpoint between opposing views.
Rather, the Golden Mean is fundamentally a rejection of extremes in favor
of moderation, a method of balancing interests that is rooted in virtue and
derived through reason. A commonly cited example: Courage is the golden
mean between rashness and cowardice.

Journalists have sometimes drawn upon this middle-ground principle in
attempts to promote fairness to all parties in ethical conflicts. One example
might be prohibiting adult-content or risqué television programming during
times when children are likely to be watching but permitting it at other
times.

Kant's Categorical Imperative

One of the giants of metaphysics, German philosopher Immanuel Kant
(1724–1804) worried that the revolutionary discoveries and theories of
Galileo, Newton, and other scientists, however stimulating they might be,
would lead society into a mechanistic world view, one that would rely upon
the laws of physics and mathematics at the expense of beliefs in free will,
morality, and personal responsibility. His ultimate moral principle was the
"categorical imperative," which helped usher in the modern era of ethical
theory. It decreed that humans should "act as if the maxim of your action
were to become through your will a universal law of nature." In other
words, we should adopt only those principles that all of society should
adopt. Before enacting a rule or law, we should ask, what would be the
result if everyone acted in this manner? In Kant's view, then, a truly moral
law is unconditional, and binding upon all members of society.

THE AGE OF ENLIGHTENMENT

The rise of the liberal[2] constitutional state was one component of a larger social and intellectual transformation which over the course of several centuries
radically altered almost every aspect of life in the Western world. Before the
toppling of the old order, medieval kings and queens had laid claim to their
thrones through heredity and through "divine right," the notion that their
monarchies were part of God's infallible plan and that they themselves were
infallible as well. But the Renaissance helped stimulate reassessments of those
feudal, authoritarian systems, and after the bloody revolutions of the 1600s
and 1700s actual political power began to shift to constitutional legislatures.

Called the Age of Reason or the Age of Enlightenment, the period from
about 1650 to 1850 was marked by intellectual vigor, breathtaking advances
in science, the rise of an increasingly influential middle class (as advocated
by philosophers such as John Locke), and a general optimism, particularly a
belief that rationality could lead humanity out of the darkness of tyranny and

> There's a huge difference between taste and ethics. . . . You can live with a taste indiscretion. Three days after you run a distasteful picture, people forget. You run an unethical picture — a picture that lies — people never forget.
> — John Long, former president, NPPA[3]

ignorance. Many of the profound thinkers of the day—among them Voltaire, Kant, Thomas Paine, and Thomas Jefferson—helped contribute to a theory of natural law that held that certain great truths are fundamental to human nature and may be deduced through pure reason, without reference to the dictates of monarchies or religions. The humanitarianism of the age is reflected in such documents as the Declaration of Independence and the Constitution of the United States, particularly its Preamble (with its references to "We the people" and "the blessings of liberty") and the Bill of Rights.

John Stuart Mill

English philosopher and economist John Stuart Mill, a late-Enlightenment thinker and reformer, was born in 1806. His father was a writer, tutor, and by all accounts a severe taskmaster who subjected his young son to excessive demands of academic achievement. John began to study Greek at age three and within five years had memorized substantial portions of the writings of Plato. By the time he was 13, he had demonstrated an impressive grasp of calculus, logic, and Latin.

Mill adopted the utilitarian philosophy of Jeremy Bentham (1748–1842), a theory often summarized as promoting the greatest good for the greatest number; that is, an action is right to the extent that it contributes to the general happiness of society. Utilitarianism is a consequentialist view: The appropriateness of an act may be judged by the goodness or badness of its consequences. Infusing utilitarianism with idealism and vitality, John Stuart Mill advocated an expansion of personal liberties, including voting rights for women. His writings, particularly the classic *On Liberty*, promoted a "marketplace of ideas" in which all voices deserved to be heard and also, of particular importance to journalists, an almost unrestricted freedom of expression.

The First Amendment

Enacted in 1791, the First Amendment to the U.S. Constitution is viewed with reverence by all informed citizens, certainly journalists. It states:

> Congress shall make no law respecting an establishment of religion, or prohibiting the free exercise thereof; or abridging the freedom of speech, or of the press, or the right of the people peaceably to assemble, and to petition the Government for a redress of grievances.

> The Preamble to the code of Ethics of the Society of Professional Journalists, as revised in September 1996, states: "Public enlightenment is the forerunner of justice and the foundation of democracy. . . . Professional integrity is the cornerstone of a journalist's credibility." The Code's four topic headings summarize journalism's ideals: Seek Truth and Report It, Minimize Harm, Act Independently, Be Accountable.[4]

These guarantees have formed the bedrock of journalistic theory and ethics throughout the nation's history, and have been extended beyond the printing press to television, radio, and other media. Freedom of expression, including freedom of the press, is thought to benefit society in several ways. It helps assure individual self-fulfillment, in keeping with Enlightenment concepts of free will and natural law. Second, it is a means to gaining truth, as explained by several Enlightenment thinkers, especially Mill. Third, it is essential to citizens' abilities to inform themselves, to investigate competing political platforms, and to other activities essential to self-governance. Finally, free expression helps maintain a reasonable balance between stability and change in society.[5]

COMPETING CONSIDERATIONS

Once a person or group agrees upon a set of ethical principles, challenges often remain simply because those principles may require interpretation on a case-by-case basis. On occasion, some of them may even conflict with each other.

The Individual versus the Group

A key goal of any ethical system is the attempt to balance the values and needs of an individual against those of another individual or those of the community, the state, or other organization. Even in political systems where personal liberties are highly valued, one's conduct is typically restricted for the greater good of the community, as when your freedom to drive your car in the manner you wish is restricted to the extent necessary to promote public safety, or when a newspaper might withhold a story containing secrets about missile systems in the belief that its publication would compromise national security.

Absolutes versus Qualifications

Ethical systems also typically entail enumerating a set of valued actions or behaviors and then providing guidelines for determining when, if ever, exceptions are tolerated. Exceptions are sometimes allowed even regarding prohibitions against the most destructive behavior, as when killing another human being is sometimes considered to be justified in the name of self-defense, the defense of others, war, or deterring crime (by executing a convicted murderer). On the other hand, a belief that killing another person is always wrong is an example of an *absolute*, a conviction that is always right and true and is never justified by extenuating circumstances, no matter how extreme.

JOURNALISTIC ETHICS

In much the same way that constitutions and laws seek to balance individual freedoms and the common good, journalistic codes of ethics attempt to balance in a moral fashion the interests of the journalist, the public, and journalistic institutions. The interests of journalists might include advancing their status, salaries, or careers; contributing to the efforts of their colleagues; and serving the public. The interests of the public include a desire to be well informed with regard to public policy, politics, health, culture, safety, the weather, sports, news at the local, regional, national and international levels, and so on. The interests of media organizations might include informing the public and, to some extent, entertaining the public (in the sense of presenting information in a compelling fashion), as well as making a profit.

All these interests may sound mutually supportive—the journalist and his or her institution want to serve the public, and the public wants to be served—but in fact they often conflict:

- In a desire to get the story, a journalist may want to interview a private citizen who does not want to be interviewed.
- In a desire to gain information from wary sources, a journalist may be tempted to conceal his or her identity or intentions.
- In telling the story, a journalist may embarrass someone who does not deserve to be embarrassed.
- In a desire to inform the public, a newspaper may run a photo of a burn victim that disturbs some readers, or a photo of a nudist that offends some readers.
- In a desire to inform the public about the progress of a crime investigation, the journalist might publish facts that enable guilty parties to escape detection.

Against the backdrop of recent mergers in which many media organizations have been subsumed into just a few mega-corporations, an issue of particular significance has emerged: Where is the line to be drawn when making a profit conflicts with serving the public?

After considering such questions, the Society of Professional Journalists, the National Press Photographers Association, and other groups have established codes of conduct that counsel journalists to serve the public; tell the truth; report the news with accuracy and objectivity; question the government; respect the privacy of individuals; protect the confidentiality of sources; avoid relationships with government, business, or other entities that might compromise objectivity or give the impression of a conflict of interest; avoid plagiarism; avoid stereotypes of race, gender, age, or ethnicity; and publish corrections to errors.

Visual Journalism Ethics

Most or all of journalism's general ethical principles have corollaries in visual journalism: serving the public, minimizing harm, and so on. In *Visual Communication: Images with Messages*,[6] Professor Paul Lester cites six ethical principles that should be applied when analyzing the meaning of photos and the motives behind them. These principles include the unconditionality of Kant's categorical imperative; the evaluation of consequences and the concept of the greater good, as advanced by the Utilitarians Bentham and Mill; the compromise and negotiation implicit in Aristotle's Golden Mean; and the humanity of the Golden Rule.

The other two principles are hedonism and the "veil of ignorance." Hedonism is an ethical philosophy founded on the belief that pleasure is the highest good. Its founder, the Greek Aristippus, believed that people should seek pleasure in the present moment with little regard for the future. Although Aristippus was concerned with intellectual pleasures such as the contemplation of meaning and reality, "hedonism" has come to refer to the pursuit of sensual and physical pleasures as well, as typified in expressions such as "eat, drink, and be merry, for tomorrow we may die." Because of its emphasis on the greater good of all people, utilitarianism is sometimes considered an Enlightenment-period expression of the original concept of hedonism.

The "veil of ignorance" was offered by John Rawls in 1971 as a method for applying principles of equality, with no class or group deserving of special privileges at the expense of another. If we look at people as if through a veil, one that obscures race, gender, ethnicity, age, and so on, their intrinsic humanity is revealed.

Manipulated Photography

In establishing ethical guidelines for new imaging technologies, we are not without precedent. Notwithstanding more than a few lapses, responsible journalists have long subscribed to a code of practice designed to protect the integrity of visual journalism. That code was captured in the National Press Photographers Association's (NPPA) 1990 statement of principle:

> As journalists we believe the guiding principle of our profession is accuracy; therefore, we believe it is wrong to alter the content of a photograph in any way that deceives the public . . . altering the editorial content of a photograph, in any degree, is a breach of the ethical standards recognized by the NPPA.[7]

A 1991 revision states that in light of emerging electronic technologies, NPPA members "reaffirm the basis of our ethics: Accurate representation is the benchmark of our profession."[8]

The Society of Professional Journalists mandates the following in its Code of Ethics:

> Never distort the content of news photos or video. Image enhancement for technical clarity is always permissible. Label montages and photo illustrations. Avoid misleading re-enactments or staged new events. If re-enactment is necessary to tell a story, label it.

SUMMARY

This chapter is far too brief to qualify even as a sketchy introduction to ethics.[9] It omits whole eras of history and ignores not only seminal figures in Western philosophy (Aquinas, Hobbes, Bacon) but also Eastern philosophy (Buddhism, Islam, Confucianism, etc.) in its entirety. The few philosophers and concepts mentioned here were selected because of their continuing influence on journalism. It is hoped, however, that the chapter provides at least a sense that the ethics of visual journalism are one tributary of a mighty river of thought and passion that flows across the eons and contains within it the insights of some of history's most creative thinkers. The next three chapters explain how some of these principles are reflected in the traditions of taking, processing, and publishing mass-media photographs.

EXPLORATIONS

1. Review Chapter 5. Discuss the photo alterations listed under the "Too Shocking" subhead in terms of Aristotle's Golden Mean.

2. In the same magazine that used an altered photo of Kate Moss on the cover (see Figure 5.1), an unaltered version appeared on an interior page; discuss these facts in terms of the Golden Mean.

3. Discuss the "political correctness" rationales presented in Chapter 5 in terms of the utilitarian principle of the greater good.

ENDNOTES

1. William Langley, "Ethics and the Bottom Line," *News Photographer* (September 1992): 58.
2. The term "liberal" is used here in reference to a political philosophy of the 18th century that reflected a belief in the freedom of political thought, the freedom of religion, free enterprise, and the importance of conscience and justice in politics.
3. "Forum Focus: Photo-journalism or Photo-fiction," a video produced by the Freedom Forum, 1101 Wilson Blvd., Arlington, Virginia 22209; 1995.
4. The SPJ's ethics guide is called *Doing Ethics in Journalism: A Handbook with Case Studies* by Jay Black, Bob Steele, and Ralph Barney (1993). For information, contact the Society at Box 77, 16 So. Jackson St., Greencastle, IN 46135-0077.

5. See Thomas I. Emerson, *Toward a General Theory of the First Amendment* (New York: Random House, 1966), 3.

6. Paul Lester, *Visual Communication: Images with Messages* (Belmont, CA: Wadsworth, 1995).

7. A Statement of Principle, 1993 NPPA Directory, p. 13; cited in Jim Gordon, "Oops! Again over Covers," *News Photographer* (September 1997): 6.

8. Passed on November 12, 1990, the statement was revised by the National Press Photographers' (NPPA) board of directors on July 3, 1991. For a discussion of efforts to develop a protocol for applying this principle, see *Protocol: NPPA Photojournalism Ethics* (Christopher Harris, ed.), presented at the annual convention of the NPPA, Washington, D.C., July 1991. Its articles include, among others: Don E. Tomlinson's "Legal and Ethical Ramifications of Computer-Assisted Photograph Manipulation"; Lou Hodges's "The Moral Imperative for Journalists"; and Bob Steele's "Protocols For Ethical Decision-Making in the Digital Age," presented at the annual convention of the NPPA, Washington, D.C., July 1991.

9. Altschull's *From Milton to McLuhan* is highly recommended as a single-volume exploration of the philosophical underpinnings of contemporary journalism. J. Herbert Altschull, *From Milton to McLuhan: The Ideas Behind American Journalism* (New York: Longman, 1990).

Chapter 7

Taking Journalistic Photographs
Traditions and Techniques

The principle is: You're not going to deceive the reader. You can violate that either beforehand by setting the picture up, or you can violate it later when you get into the computer by changing the content of the picture. In both cases it's the same principle. You don't want to deceive the reader, because once you do that you lose credibility.

—John Long[1]

PHOTOS THAT "MEAN" WHAT THEY "SAY"

It is pointless to ask whether posing or staging a mass-media photo is wrong unless we know its context. Who will be viewing the photo, and in what publishing environment? Is it a journalistic photo? If so, does it indeed reflect reality the way viewers would reasonably expect? In other words, does it "mean" what it "says"?

It would not surprise readers of the morning newspaper to learn that the international summit conference covered on the front page was not actually conducted outdoors, with the various heads of state standing shoulder to shoulder on the steps of a government building and all looking at a camera at the same moment. Readers would recognize and accept a photo of such a scene for what it is: a setup, a group portrait. Informing readers that the subjects had posed for the camera would be unnecessary. No one attempts to mislead readers in such cases, and indeed readers' assumptions are correct; such photos mean what they say. The posing of subjects may inform or qualify the reader's expectation of reality, but it does not violate it.

The pumpkin and corn meticulously arranged in the picture accompanying a newspaper feature on Thanksgiving table settings; skis and boots placed just so for a magazine article on sporting goods; the two peace-treaty signatories holding their ceremonial handshake long enough for flashbulbs to pop; the photographer taking the fourth-grade class picture asking the taller kids to stand in the back row—in such cases we know the photographer did not chance upon a random scene and simply click the shutter. Even

> Photography is a human act, and therefore subjective, a selective act, and therefore interpretive. . . . By deciding what's interesting or important enough to photograph, selecting a position, pointing the camera in a certain direction, leaving some things in and others out, and deciding when to trip the shutter, a photographer edits the universe of space and time, recording not absolute truth but a personal vision of reality.
> —Arthur Goldsmith[2]

without disclosure of the circumstances, all these images mean what they say. Our recognition of their being arranged scenes is part of our grasping their relationship to reality, their meaning.

THE "MOMENT"

What is the expectation of reality, however, when journalistic photos are not clearly posed, are not obvious setups? Such photos carry an implied promise that they, too, mean what they say. They are assumed to have captured objects or events that existed in real time and space, to a meaningful extent independent of the clicking of the shutter. If a journalistic photo presents a compelling slice of action—perhaps even what the great French photographer Henri Cartier-Bresson called "the decisive moment"—its meaning and value are found not only in its subject matter but also in its immediacy or spontaneity, its evidence of the photographer's persistence or luck in being at the right place at the right instant. It violates our expectations if we learn that the scene "captured" by a supposedly candid photo was neither spontaneous nor mostly independent of the camera but was instead staged by the photographer—or never happened at all.

WHEN THE SHUTTER SNAPS

Before addressing how a photo might be processed and published, let's look to an earlier stage, the circumstances under which it was taken. The following are some of the relevant questions:

- Was the photo spontaneous or planned?
- Did the photographer shoot what he or she saw upon arriving at the scene, or did he or she pose, place, or rearrange any elements?
- How significant are aspects of the scene or event that were ignored or overlooked by the photographer?[3]
- If it is a photo of people, did they know they were being photographed?

> Photographers show us what they want to, framing the image depending on what story they want to tell. But there is something about the immediacy of a photograph that allows us to suspend our doubts and accept it as unmediated reality.
>
> —Sara Sklaroff[4]

- What was their relationship to the photographer? Was the photographer a friend, a passerby, a news professional on assignment, a self-employed professional aiming to please the subjects (his or her clients)?
- Did the subjects alter their behavior, even slightly, because of the presence of the camera?
- Are they looking at the camera, thereby alerting viewers to their awareness of being photographed?
- Might the taking of the photo have been affected by the photographer's gender, race, or social standing; his or her conscious or subconscious tastes, philosophies, or agendas?
- Given that some photos are easier to sell than others, what was the effect of commercial considerations?

"SOFT FEATURE" PHOTOS: POSING AND STAGING

Veteran newspaper photographer Norman Zeisloft was fired from The St. Petersburg *Evening Independent* after stage-managing a photo of spectators at a baseball game. One spectator was photographed after writing—at Zeisloft's suggestion—the words "Yeah Eckerd" on the soles of his bare feet, which were propped up on a low wall and faced the camera. The photographer said in his defense: "We set up pictures for society and club news, recipe contest winners, ribbon-cutting and ground-breaking ceremonies, award shots and enterprise features."[5]

Such photos are often lumped in a class of "soft feature" imagery, as distinguished from images of wars, natural disasters, political events—so-called hard news. This distinction may render their ethical standards less rigorous. Certainly, Zeisloft's transgression seems relatively innocuous compared to faking, say, a compromising photo of a political candidate.

And yet, as evidenced by Zeisloft's firing, even "soft feature" photos carry at least some implication of veracity; they have rules, even if certain standards (regarding posing, for example) may be relatively lenient. Readers accept posing as natural and ethical in journalistic portraits and group photos. We know the subjects are aware of the camera; after all, they are typically looking at it when the picture is taken.[6]

But Zeisloft went beyond witnessing an event and posing its elements; he actually conceived the scene himself and suggested it to his subjects.[7]

> For all the crisp realism they seem to offer, photographs have a funny way of playing tricks with memory. From the kinds of pictures we take to the ones we choose to display, photos are much like family history: What really happened is often a matter of interpretation.
>
> — Emily Sohn[8]

Unless informed to the contrary, a newspaper reader's reasonable assumption would be that it was the spectator's idea to paint words on his feet, that the photographer happened to come upon an amusing scene that he captured on film. But that is not what happened. The photo did not mean what it said.

What lesson can be learned from the Zeisloft case? Simply this: Journalistic photos must be authentic. Even if they entail a bit of posing that readers are sure to recognize (as in the examples discussed above—the heads of state, the class picture, etc.), and even if they are "soft" rather than "hard" news, ethical journalistic photos must mean what they say.

We might imagine circumstances in which momentarily fooling readers might be ethical, as in a piece of visual satire, an illustration for a story on optical illusions, or some other what-you-see-is-not-what-you-get concoction. But absent such unusual circumstances, and absent full disclosure, any posing or staging in a journalistic photo that does not conform to reasonable assumptions will dupe viewers. Publication of that photo is an ethical lapse that risks a loss of credibility.

AFTER THE FACT: HOFFMAN AND CRUISE

With software we can now "pose subjects" or "stage events" after the fact. Of course, we could always do it in the darkroom, but now we can do it more easily, less expensively, and more realistically. Indeed, we can pose subjects without even telling them. As editor in chief David Schonauer wrote in *American Photo*, "In the digital age, nearly any impossible pairing can be manufactured. All that's needed is a decent computer, state-of-the-art software (which now costs about $600), and someone with a good deal of skill to bring it off."[9]

As mentioned in Chapter 4, Dustin Hoffman and Tom Cruise appeared together offscreen in a *Newsweek* "photo" that accompanied a story about the movie *Rain Man* (Figure 4.5). The image appeared to "say" this: Here are the two actors side by side; the shot may be spontaneous, or then again it may be a "photo op" (an arranged photo opportunity), but either way the subjects are smiling and apparently enjoying each other's company.

As it turned out, the image was a composite. The actors were photographed at different places, different times. Without disclosure of the manipulation, the photo did not mean what it said. Readers' expectations of reality—even if qualified by accepting the image as a photo op—were violated. Its appearance in a news magazine, of all places, intensified its failure to conform to reader expectations.

PHOTOJOURNALISM AND DOCUMENTARY PHOTOGRAPHY

The terms "photojournalism" and "documentary photography" are sometimes treated as if they are interchangeable, but they are not. As Professor James D. Kelly explains, "The difference has to do with photographic intention. For a photojournalist, the intention is to present the news 'objectively.'

FIGURE 7.1.   Lewis Hine's compelling photos, such as this 1908 image, helped inspire the movement to protect children with revised labor laws.

Photojournalistic Agendas

To assert that photography can reflect reality in a compelling way does not require us to deny its interpretive aspects, as suggested here by Dr. Bill Ryan, University of Oregon School of Journalism and Communication. Dr. Ryan has extensively researched Farm Security Administration (FSA) photojournalism. Founded in 1937 as a component of President Franklin Roosevelt's New Deal, the FSA helped farmers buy needed equipment.

There is a kind of quiet sanctity we place on documentary photography, and along with that often comes the assumption that the work is objective. Documentary photographers — particularly social documentarians — have a personal point of view and sometimes a specific agenda. Jacob Riis [1849–1914] was hellbent to effect social change. He was outraged over the horrendous living conditions that awaited immigrants in New York City's slums. His photography was very subjective, and his mission (which was both political and social) was to stimulate action against a system that allowed such indignity and inhumanity to exist.

Essentially, Lewis Hine [1874–1940] picked up where Riis left off, also adopting a philosophy about using photography as a means to effect social change. He followed immigrant Americans from Ellis Island to the slums of New York City and into the work place, where he discovered an unexpected atrocity, one he spent much of his life trying to eliminate: the exploitation of children as laborers. Hine's work was instrumental in establishing child labor laws.

Roy Emerson Stryker, director of the historical division of the Farm Security Administration, basically orchestrated much of the work of his illustrious photographers. Although he wanted to eliminate the causes of poverty that were strangling rural America, his main charge was to win support for a wide array of social programs. Along with directives to his photographers came shooting scripts — many of which detailed whom to shoot and where. The FSA imagery is generally heralded as the single greatest photo-documentary project ever; however, it is probably also one of the government's greatest public relations campaigns.

So, along with the outward forms of manipulation or photo editing — camera angle, cropping, or selecting a single image from a group — there is an inward or perhaps less physical touch on the imagery. It lies in the hearts of the photographers and often in the minds and agendas of those who direct the photographers.

FIGURE 7.2. The Farm Security Administration set out to document the Great Depression and win support for a wide array of social programs. The results were lasting — and haunting — images, such as Dorothea Lange's "Migrant Mother."

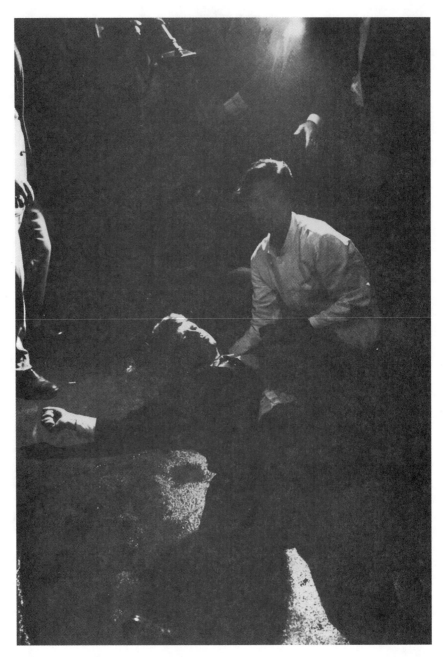

FIGURE 7.3.   Presidential candidate and Senator Robert Kennedy lay dying moments after being shot in Los Angeles in 1968. The vulnerability of all people — powerful figures and ordinary citizens — as well as a nation's grief and shock are all captured in this unforgettable image.

FIGURE 7.4. When Egyptian President Anwar Sadat was assassinated by religious militants in 1981, photojournalism provided a harrowing, you-are-there glimpse of the violence.

> Should portraits be held to a lower standard? Not in my opinion. If anything, perhaps [portraiture] should be elevated, given its legacy and rich potential. Some of the finest and most memorable photography we have is portraiture.
> — Bill Ryan, University of Oregon[10]

The documentarian makes no such pretense. Both arrive at a truth, but one is immediate and necessarily contemporaneous with events. The other is reflective and most often separated from actual events by enough time that it is no longer newsworthy. Both are nonfiction, however."[11] In other words, both carry the implications of authenticity referred to in this chapter.

A WORD ABOUT GEAR

When listing the various qualifications to photography's "objectivity," we should not overlook choices of equipment. After all, such subjective decisions can result in arguably misleading photos, as when depth of field seems to reveal that foreground and background elements are closer or further apart than they actually are, or when a wide angle lens is used to exaggerate scale or distort perspective.

Usually, however, standard techniques—choice of f-stop, choice of exposure, perhaps the use of a fish-eye lens or black-and-white film—pose no threat to credibility because consumers recognize, for example, that a fish-eye is a "special effect," that reality is not literally black and white.

SUMMARY

The extent to which a photo truly "captures" an event, person, or scene depends upon many considerations, including the effect of the photographer's presence, his or her intentions or biases, and his or her relationship to the subjects. In any case, ethical journalistic photos (whether film-based or digital) mean what they say. Given their context, they reflect reality in a way that conforms to viewers' reasonable assumptions. Even if their standards may vary in regard to the appropriateness of posing, "hard" and "soft" journalistic photos all carry implications of authenticity.

EXPLORATIONS

1. When examining a wedding photo or a typical family album picture, what assumptions do you make about the circumstances under which the photo was taken, and about the relationship between the

Should portraits be held to a lower standard? How about a <u>different</u> standard? A portrait, assuming it is not portrayed as a candid shot, is meant to be an artful depiction. As long as that is made clear to the public, that is fine. Should consumer magazines have different standards? Depends what they are doing. If they are portraying a picture as representing reality, then they need to conform to the best-depiction standard [i.e., they depict external reality as closely as possible].

— Deni Elliott, University of Montana[12]

photographer and the subjects? How do those assumptions differ in regard to journalistic photos? Would such distinctions affect your opinion of whether manipulating a given photo is ethical?

2. Does the term "staged" carry the same connotation as "posed," or does it suggest that something was faked in order to mislead viewers? Would it apply to a typical photographic portrait? To entertainment or political "photo ops" (arranged photo opportunities)? When might a posed or staged photo be unethical?

3. Consider two scenarios, both involving a newspaper's coverage of a human interest story in which the mayor rescues her next-door neighbor's kitten from a tree. In the first, the photographer comes upon the scene as it unfolds and asks the mayor to descend a few rungs on the ladder, to hold the kitten a certain way, and to look into the camera. In the second, the photographer comes upon the scene minutes after the rescue and asks the mayor to reenact the rescue for the camera. The resulting photos look identical. What are the differences, if any, regarding the "reality" they capture? Do both photos "mean what they say," as the phrase is used in this chapter?

4. On the 1992 presidential campaign trail, CNN videographer William Langley reported that he photographed Dan Quayle waving from the back of a train "to the passing trees and telephone poles. There were no people in sight." Later, in a small North Carolina town, Langley aimed his camera at a group of people waving to the passing train. Back at CNN, the shots were edited together, "leaving the impression that the vice president routinely waved to throngs of people from the back of his train. This was not the case."[13] Did the images meet the reasonable expectations of viewers who encountered them on television? Was their use ethical in the context of a news broadcast?

5. Consider a back-to-school photo for the local paper in which a particular lens is selected to bring a young student into sharper focus against the backdrop of her school. Now consider a newspaper

article about the hazards of radioactive waste, accompanied by a picture taken with a telephoto lens that seems to reveal that neighborhood homes are closer to a nuclear power plant than they actually are. Assume there is no disclosure of the camera technique in either case. Ethically speaking, are the techniques of equal significance?

6. Imagine three scenarios in which a photo appears in a daily newspaper's "City & Neighborhood" section:
   - In the first, the photographer sees two men piling sandbags on a makeshift flood levee and captures their activity on film.
   - In the second, he sees them engaged in the activity and asks them to repeat it to allow time for loading the film and positioning the camera.
   - In both scenarios, the photo and the caption ("Local residents help out in the face of advancing floodwaters") are identical.
   - In the third scenario, the photographer asks the two men to pose by the levee; they stand shoulder to shoulder and look into the lens as the shutter snaps. The caption: "Biff Jones and Bob Smith were among volunteers who worked on a levee in the face of advancing floodwaters." Ethically, do the scenarios differ?

ENDNOTES

1. "Forum Focus: Photo-journalism or Photo-fiction," a video produced by the Freedom Forum, 1101 Wilson Blvd., Arlington, Virginia 22209; 1995.
2. Arthur Goldsmith, "Photos Always Lied," *Popular Photography* (November 1991): 68.
3. Sometimes visual journalists intentionally "overlook" certain aspects of a scene in order to influence viewers' perceptions of the image. For example, in his acclaimed 1934 documentary *Man of Aran*, Robert Flaherty meticulously positioned his cameras so that no power lines appeared in his depictions of "primitive" villages. A. David Gordon and John Michael Kittross, *Controversies in Media Ethics* (New York: Longman, 1999), 281.
4. Sara Sklaroff, "The Timeless Moment," *U.S. News & World Report* (July 9–16, 2001): 25.
5. Paul Lester, *Photojournalism: An Ethical Approach* (Hillsdale, NJ: Lawrence Erlbaum Assoc., 1991), 115. Lester cited a report by Professor Jim Gordon, editor of *News Photographer* magazine.
6. Professor Lester summarized: "To simulate color in daguerreotypes, photo retouchers with brushes and inks added red to cheeks and blue to dresses. Before invention of the halftone process, skillful engravers regularly altered the content of photographs. . . . wedding and portrait photographers remove unwanted warts and wrinkles. . . . Advertising art directors customarily combine parts of pictures, change colors, and create fantasy images to attract customers. People are well aware of such practices and knowingly suspend belief when looking at portrait and advertising images." Paul Lester, *Visual Communication: Images with Messages* (Belmont, CA: Wadsworth, 1995), 266–67.
7. Professor Lester concluded: "Zeisloft, at 61 years old, may have been influenced by the stage managing techniques that photographers had used several years earlier because of their bulky cameras. . . . Norman Zeisloft's sin was not realizing that the ethics of stage-managed pictures had changed." Lester, *Photojournalism*, 115–18.
8. Emily Sohn, "Want a Memory? Say 'Cheese,' " *U.S. News & World Report* (July 9–16, 2001): 71.
9. David Schonauer, "The Future of Photography 1997," *American Photo* (November/December 1997): 45.
10. Professor Ryan is a photographer, graphic designer, author, poet, and award-winning educator at the University of Oregon's School of Journalism and Communication. From an e-mail correspondence with the author, fall 1998.

11. Professor Kelly teaches photojournalism, graphics, and new communication technologies at Southern Illinois University at Carbondale. He is also the editor of *Visual Communication Quarterly*. From an e-mail correspondence with the author, fall 1999.

12. Deni Elliott is a professor in both the Department of Philosophy and the School of Journalism at the University of Montana, as well as the director of the University's Practical Ethics Center. From an e-mail correspondence with the author, fall 1998.

13. William Langley, "Ethics and the Bottom Line," *News Photographer* (September 1992): 58.

Chapter 8

Processing Journalistic Photographs
Keeping It Real

If . . . consumers . . . decide to revoke the credibility they have bestowed on photojournalism . . . it will be because the processes of photojournalism were at some point so revolutionized that photographic reality could no longer be trusted to be the result.

—Don Tomlinson[1]

Film-based photographs must be developed and processed before they are ready to be considered for publication, and these steps are routine and ethically insignificant in most cases. Accepted processing techniques are within the "grammar" of photography; that is, they are responsible practices that serve to clarify, focus, or otherwise fine-tune an image. On the other hand, altering meaning or "content" is ethically problematical.

PHOTOGRAPHIC CONTENT

"Content" refers to subject matter, not merely the foremost object or person in a photo but details as well. In a picture of a girl on a horse, the girl, the horse, and the rest of the scene—the barn in the background, flowers in the foreground, sky, clouds, a buzzing fly, every blade of grass—are all "content." Large or small, important or relatively unimportant, if it existed at the scene and was captured on film, it is content.

This concept is important, because many codes and policies distinguish using chemical, mechanical, or digital means to alter content (typically considered unethical) from merely enhancing what's already there (often considered ethical). As we saw in Chapter 6, for example, the Code of Ethics of the Society of Professional Journalists reads in part: "Never distort the content of news photos or video. Image enhancement for technical clarity is always permissible."

Almost as soon as we make this distinction, however, its limitations become apparent. Removing a pimple, lightening a shadow, intensifying contrast between objects—all could be said to "alter content." One might argue that alterations to content begin even before the picture is snapped, with the selection of shutter speed, lens, filters, etc. Admittedly neither airtight nor comprehensive, the "content versus enhancement" distinction is nevertheless useful, as we will see.

TRADITIONAL TECHNIQUES

Let us examine traditional techniques intended to preserve photographic content.

Cleaning and Repairing Negatives

Negatives in less than pristine condition can be cleaned up in the darkroom. Scratches can be concealed, fingerprints removed; even the ravages of fire and water, if not too severe, can be repaired. Such improvements are ethical and within the grammar of journalistic photo processing.

Cropping

Mass-media photos are often trimmed or "cropped" to eliminate what the photographer or editor considers visual trivia and to highlight important elements (Figure 8.1). Note that "cropping" refers to reducing the borders of an image, rather than removing elements from within the borders. We can imagine an example of unethical cropping, as when essential elements are eliminated and the remaining image is misleading. Otherwise, readers know that a whole world exists outside the frame of a picture, and appropriate cropping does not mislead them. The practice has long been within the bounds of photography's grammar.

Even when a highly skilled darkroom technician creates an altered photograph that can fool a well-trained expert, examining the negative (if possible) will immediately betray the manipulation. To a great extent, this technical limitation on manipulation, coupled with media professionals' ethical practice, has guaranteed, to a large extent, the authenticity of documentary photographs published in print media in the pre-digital-imaging era.

— Edgar Huang[2]

FIGURE 8.1. Cropping is a compositional tool that continues the process begun when the photographer frames the photo and enables him or her to isolate important elements.

Dodging and Burning

Dodging (selective shading) and burning (or "burning in"—increasing density with extra exposure) are employed to improve a photo's contrast, to enhance its clarity, and so on (Figure 8.2). Suppose that in a photo a child's face is shadowed by her hat; lightening the face a bit improves detail, better serving the reader and leaving the photo's "reality" uncompromised. Like cropping, this traditional practice would not be considered unethical by professionals. For example, the Hearst student journalism competition rules (see box in Chapter 13) expressly permit dodging and burning.

Color Correction

If you have compared different photos of a painting to the original, or even to each other, you may have noticed significant color variations. The reds in one photo look orange in another; blues look violet. Even when the printer's aim is to reproduce the original as faithfully as possible, an array of factors can contribute to perceived color shifts, including the temperatures and

FIGURE 8.2. Long-accepted darkroom techniques enable processors to improve a photo's clarity, to correct areas that are too dark or too light, or to highlight certain aspects, as revealed here by uncorrected (above) and corrected (opposite page) prints of the same negative.

chemistry of the development process, exposure times, the type of paper (composition, thickness, coating), the way paper reflects light compared to a projected slide or an onscreen computer image, the reproduction's age and exposure to sunlight, and so on.

The grammar of photography allows fine adjustments to color in order to better match the object or scene. Going far beyond that standard (changing blue skies to red, for example), while accepted in artistic creations, would not be appropriate in journalistic photos.

Airbrushing, Cosmetic Touch-Ups

The Associated Press limits retouching to "removal of normal scratches and dust spots," but other professionals have for many decades gone much further, using airbrushes or other tools to "improve" images, particularly portraits. As we might expect, these standards vary considerably depending upon the content of the photo (hard news versus a feature portrait, for example), and the type of publication (daily newspapers versus celebrity-oriented consumer magazines, etc.). So-called cosmetic retouching is addressed in Chapter 17.

FIGURE 8.2.   Continued

The concept of the <u>moment</u> is sacrosanct to photojournalism. I believe that this idea is how people today define visual "truth." We photographers, and our readers, have all come to believe that once the shutter has been tripped and light has been exposed on film, we no longer have the right to change the content of the photograph other than in mechanical ways (such as a little contrast control or dodging and burning). It is the violation of this concept that has made the computer the great evil thing some have been saying it is. However, the computer is neither good nor bad. It is amoral, not immoral. It is merely a useful tool.

—John Long, former president, NPPA[3]

SUMMARY

As we saw in the previous chapter, setting up or posing a mass-media photo may be ethical so long as the image means what it says and readers are not duped. Similarly, post-exposure processing is ethical as well, so long as it does not distort content. Cleaning negatives, correcting colors, cropping, dodging, and burning all have been considered within the grammar of accepted practices. While some of these methods can be carried to extremes in order to distort the results, their typical application simply allows a photo to more effectively reflect the reality of a scene.

EXPLORATIONS

1. Bring to class a photo on the front page of your daily newspaper or the cover of a recent news magazine. How might it have been treated during processing? Consider cropping, darkening, and lightening. Can you imagine an alteration that would have diminished or destroyed its authenticity?

2. Imagine ways in which cropping might be used to mislead readers. Consider photographs of (a) your own room, home, or apartment; (b) a street scene in your community; (c) a gathering of your family or friends; and (d) a crowd attending a political speech.

3. Imagine ways in which color alteration might be used to mislead viewers. Consider photographs of (a) professional models in an ad for beauty products; (b) a newspaper photo of a political candidate surrounded by supporters; (c) exterior and interior photos of a home appearing in a magazine; (d) nature photos.

> When a photograph becomes synthesis, fantasy rather than
> reportage, then the whole purpose of the photograph dies.
> —Jan Adkins, former associate art director, _National Geographic_[4]

ENDNOTES

1. Professor Tomlinson teaches at the school of journalism at Texas A&M. Don E. Tomlinson, "Digi-texed Television News: The Beginning of the End for Photographic Reality in Photojournalism," _Business & Professional Ethics Journal 11_ (spring 1992): 52.
2. Edgar Shaohua Huang, "Readers' Perception of Digital Alteration and Truth-Value in Documentary Photographs," submitted in partial fulfillment for a Ph.D. degree, School of Journalism, Indiana University (October 1999): 6.
3. From an e-mail correspondence with the author, fall 1998.
4. J.D. Lasica, "Photographs That Lie: The Ethical Dilemma of Digital Retouching," _Washington Journalism Review_ (June 1989): 25.

Chapter 9

Publishing Journalistic Photographs
Context and Viewer Preconceptions

When we look at a photograph, we are faced with only one version of reality and what we understand is only one of its given truths. In reading a photograph we do many things. We absorb information, we impose meaning, and we experience emotion. This is a dynamic process in which the picture depends on the culture of the photographer and the culture of the viewer.

—Pedro Meyer[1]

PRIVATE USES VERSUS MASS MEDIA

Having examined the taking and processing of photos, we now turn to the publishing environment in which they appear, elements that accompany a photo such as text or other images, the awareness or preconceptions of audiences, and other factors that affect how viewers perceive images. Together, these elements contribute to photographic context.

Imagine a snapshot of a young couple snuggling romantically at a candlelit dinner on their honeymoon. Few people would object if, before the image is framed and placed on the mantelpiece at home, it undergoes alterations such as color correction, lightening a shaded area for better visibility, or cropping out the hovering waiter.

On the other hand, suppose the man is a public figure—a congressional candidate, for example—and suppose the image of his bride is replaced with the image of, say, a demonstrably affectionate Dallas Cowboys cheerleader in uniform. Clearly, the image has been fictionalized. If the couple wants to share it with friends or include it in their photo album as a gag, that is their business. But if it is published in the mass media and passed off as anything other than fantasy or satire, its ethical shortcomings are apparent.

As this example readily reveals, the ethics of an altered image entail not only the nature of the alteration but also the photo's use, that is, its environment.

PHOTOGRAPHIC ENVIRONMENT

More complex questions of context include the publication's perceived approach to its subject matter: academic, irreverent, or whatever the case may be. Because ethical journalistic photos reflect reality in the manner readers expect, it only makes sense to recognize that such expectations shift drastically with shifts in context. Absent clear signals to the contrary, a photo alongside a news story in a daily newspaper carries with it a promise of sorts, an assurance that the image, like the text, is journalism. It is nonfiction. It is real. As we will see, those standards may slip or even disappear altogether when photos appear in other contexts.

CAN A PHOTO BE UNETHICAL?

We hear of "ethical" or "unethical" photos, but these terms are simplistic, useful mainly as shorthand for more complex assessments. Most people agree that while words can be used in unethical ways, words themselves are ethically neutral. Are photographs any different? Granted, some people may believe that certain photos are inherently immoral (for example, child pornography), just as some may believe that certain words are inherently immoral (obscenities, perhaps, or racial epithets). But aside from such extremes, the ethics of a photo, even a manipulated one, cannot be judged apart from its use.

More specifically, the decisions we make about how we compose, set up, process, or use a photo can be ethical or unethical, appropriate or inappropriate. Our judgment can be good or bad. But like a word, a given photo is itself ethically neutral. Consequently, sound ethical judgments must address not only the content or even the manipulation of a photo but also what might be called its larger meaning.

It is not necessary for us to agree on the one and only "larger meaning" a photo might have. After all, a photo can mean different things to different people, or even different things to one person at different times. But as we attempt to distinguish unethical alterations from the kinds of posing and enhancements accepted throughout photography's history, let us remember

> The combination of text and photographs is, indeed, the guiding principle and single most important characteristic of photojournalism. . . . [Former Life magazine editor Wilson Hicks] contends that the basic unit of photojournalism is not the gritty hard-news picture standing alone, but photographs and text printed together. In this informational mix, picture content matters less than the manner in which the picture is used.
> —Michael L. Carlebach, The Origins of Photojournalism in America[2]

that a photo is not merely an image bound within a frame but rather one element of a process that begins in the mind of the photographer and ends in the mind of the viewer.

PHOTO EDITING

The taking and processing of photos are only two of the stages between the reality of an event and its visual portrayal in mass media. Writers and photographers encounter a flood of facts and images, only a tiny portion of which appear in the work they turn in to their bosses. Some degree of subjectivity must affect their assessments of which facts and images are significant and which may be ignored. Subjectivity further affects the process as story editors and photo editors revise, recast, and arrange the work prior to publication.

Regarding the taking of journalistic photos, we asked about the significance of aspects of the scene or event that were overlooked by the photographer. Regarding processing, we asked whether content was altered. Now, at the editing stage, we might consider aspects of context such as the following:

- What "picture of reality" might have been conveyed by the photos that were taken and processed but never published?
- How representative are the published photos of the actual events or scenes they purport to have "captured"?
- To what extent might photo editing have been affected by an editor's gender, race, or social standing; his or her conscious or subconscious tastes, philosophies, or agendas?
- Given that some photos sell more papers or magazines than others,[3] what was the effect of commercial considerations upon the selection of images?

TEXT AND OTHER ELEMENTS

The context of a photo also includes its placement, its size, the wording and tone of its caption and accompanying text, and its relationship to surrounding elements—headlines, pull-quotes, other images, and so on, all of which may provide clues as to the photo's purported reality. The same is true for other

> The competition is so fierce that magazines on the newsstand have about three to five seconds to attract the potential buyer. Therefore, this competition requires near flawless cover photographs, and that affects picture editing decisions.
> — Edgar Huang[4]

To be sure, today's readers see through jaded eyes. What's more, they hold extravagant expectations that are fed daily by the media — pseudo-events, celebrity gossip, and entertainment. They see very little documentary. Mind you, good photo-documentary has not gone away. There is some wonderful work; unfortunately, very little appears in mainstream publications as it once did. Frankly, though, I am more concerned with agendas of editors and the manipulation that might involve than with digital photography per se. It is, after all, publishers and editors who control publications and steer the content of those forums.

— Bill Ryan, University of Oregon[5]

visual media, such as television, for example. When the voice of a news anchor describes a scene, viewers presume that the film they are watching at that moment depicts the same scene. In the 1960s, when one New York television station purported to provide daily coverage of the Vietnam war but in fact reran stock footage without disclaimers, viewers were misled.[6]

VIEWER PRECONCEPTIONS

Once photos are published, still other aspects of context come into play. Whether our audiences are readers, listeners or viewers, all journalists ask, Who *are* these media consumers, exactly? What knowledge or biases do they bring to the table, and how should those preconceptions or expectations affect what we cover, and how we cover it? Some audiences possess special knowledge or are more sophisticated than others. They may recognize certain aspects of a photo, including its relationship to actual events, that may not be recognized by others. Certainly, any assumptions about viewers' perceptions of a photo could affect decisions regarding its ethics. (Seasoned media professionals admit that despite their use of sophisticated surveys and analysis of reader mail and other feedback, assessing the attitudes and beliefs of readers often entails plenty of assumptions and more than a little guesswork.)

We might also consider how readers might be predisposed or "primed" by events and media coverage to "read" or interpret a photo in a certain way. In such cases, misleading photos may seem to be logical follow-ups to credible accounts of actual events. As the editors of *U.S. News & World Report* wrote in 2001, "Photographs are capable of stopping time and capturing the essence of events across cultures. They can be seductive, encouraging us to endow them with stories of our own—assumptions that are incomplete at best and wrong at worst."[7]

READERS' AWARENESS OF RETOUCHING

A most welcome addition to the scholarly literature on photo manipulation is Edgar Huang's 1999 study, "Readers' Perception of Digital Alteration and Truth-Value in Documentary Photographs." Building to some degree upon the work of Professor Shiela Reaves, the project employed a mailed survey and extensive interviews in an attempt to answer two broad questions: To what extent do readers of print news media accept digital alterations in documentary photos, and how is their trust in digitally altered documentary photos related to their understandings of truth and reality?

Dr. Huang concluded that some types of alterations could gain high levels of acceptance among readers while nevertheless holding the potential for alienating those same readers in the long run. He wrote: "They regard photographic illustrations appearing in places like news magazine covers as pure art, feature photographs as semi-art, and semi-news and hard news photographs as factual . . . the respondents prefer that editors try their best not to alter images, especially news images."[8]

SUMMARY

Ethical journalistic photos conform to reasonable viewer expectations. Those expectations, in turn, can be influenced not only by a photo's content but also by its surrounding elements, the nature of the publication, viewers' preconceptions, the manner in which the photo seems to conform to (or to contradict) various stereotypes, and other aspects of context.

In the next chapter we will ask whether standards should differ between news magazines and general interest magazines; "features" and "articles"; magazine covers and interior photos; or print and online media.

EXPLORATIONS

1. *Newsweek*'s cover of O.J. Simpson (Figure 9.1) was cited favorably in many articles critical of *Time*'s O.J. Simpson cover, which appeared the same week and was excoriated as racist and legally prejudicial. This image is certainly less manipulated than *Time*'s, but is it "unmanipulated"? Simpson's hairline appears to have been drawn with the digital equivalent of the artist's black pencil; is this an example of "processing," or "alteration," or perhaps "manipulation"? What are the ethical connotations of each description? Can the ethics of this image be judged without considering the implication of its accompanying cover text? In other words, can its context be ignored?

2. Bring to class some examples of photos appearing in newspapers or news magazines. Be prepared to discuss how the publishing

FIGURE 9.1. This <u>Newsweek</u> cover was cited favorably in many articles critical of <u>Time</u>'s O.J. Simpson cover. Looking more closely, however, is this photo unmanipulated?

environment (the name, type and reputation of the publication, aspects of surrounding text, other elements on the page) might affect how you perceive the photo. Imagine differences in photographic environment that might change your perception of the image.

3. Bring to class photos or photolike images appearing in satirical or overtly implausible contexts. Can you imagine circumstances in which these images would be appropriate in a newspaper or news

magazine? If so, would such use require a disclaimer or an explanatory caption?

4. Examine a group of photos taken at a single event—either separate prints or images on a proof sheet. If you had to select only one picture to accompany a journalistic report of the event, which one would it be? Why? What sorts of differences might be implied by using a different picture?

ENDNOTES

1. Stephen Beale, "Digital Photography & The Visual Truth," *Digital Imaging* (January/February 1994): 12.
2. Michael L. Carlebach, *The Origins of Photojournalism in America* (Washington and London: Smithsonian Institution Press, 1992), 1–2.
3. It is an article of faith among magazine editors that the primary sales tool of any issue is its cover—not merely the topic it specifies but also its design and illustration. At practically any publication offered for sale at newsstands or other single-copy outlets, the sales success of every issue is regularly analyzed in comparison to its cover design. For example, see Sammye Johnson and Patricia Prijatel, "Cover Hits and Misses at *Time*," in their book *Magazine Publishing* (Lincolnwood, IL: NTC/ Contemporary, 1999): 317.
4. Huang, 41.
5. From an e-mail correspondence with the author, fall 1998.
6. A. David Gordon and John Michael Kittross, *Controversies in Media Ethics* (New York: Longman, 1999), 282.
7. *U.S. News & World Report* (July 9–16, 2001): 28.
8. Edgar Shaohua Huang, "Readers' Perception of Digital Alteration and Truth-Value in Documentary Photographs," submitted in partial fulfillment for a Ph.D. degree, School of Journalism, Indiana University, October 1999, 183.

IV

Developing a Protocol

Chapter 10

The "Nonfiction Photographic Environment"

A Range of Implied Authenticity

The integrity of each photo is critical. You can't compromise one without raising a question about all.

—Alex MacLeod, *The Seattle Times*[1]

The digital age presents us with challenges at once profound and exhilarating. How can we apply limitless image-processing technologies in creative and commercial ways—without fracturing the credibility that is the foundation of our profession? Is it even possible? Or will we Photoshop ourselves out of a job? In a media environment awash in false yet photorealistic imagery, can journalists maintain a fortress of credibility around real images, isolating them in the public mind from "photo-illustrations" and other contrivances?

Part III examined principles of journalistic ethics, as well as the conventions of taking, processing, and publishing photographs. We can now draw upon those traditions in formulating guidelines for the responsible, credibility-preserving implementation of digital image processing. Part IV, the essence of this book, is intended to sharpen our focus and to assist in protocol development, not by providing all the answers but by proposing a method of asking questions:

- First, this chapter outlines the nonfiction photographic environment, a category broader than "photojournalism" or "hard news," and one that embraces a range of implied authenticity.
- The following chapters offer various tests that reveal whether a photo meets the reader's "Qualified Expectation of Reality," or "QER," offered here as the essential standard for identifying "photofiction."

- The text goes on to address appropriate disclosure of photofiction, and the implications of "cosmetic" retouching.
- Chapter 18 explains how to apply the guidelines in a brief list of questions and steps, and the book concludes with an exploration of the future of journalistic photography in Chapters 19 and 20.

Taken together, these chapters offer an approach to assessing the ethics of an altered mass-media photograph. At every step, choices must be made and judgments rendered. Where students or professionals draw the line will depend upon their own perceptions of their responsibilities.

RE-CATEGORIZING IMAGES

It is an uncertain environment of ubiquitous image manipulation, diminished faith in mass media, and justifiable viewer skepticism that visual journalists face as they attempt to preserve their credibility. How can they do it? One preliminary step is to better define the category of mass-media images that carry implications of authenticity. This chapter argues that photocredibility's survival requires applying ethical standards to a category broader than "photojournalism" or "hard news."[2]

This chapter also suggests that for ethical purposes, distinctions between newspapers, magazines, and other media have begun to outlive their usefulness. In an age in which the forms and structures of nonfiction communication diverge and recombine into innumerable permutations, why should ethical guidelines turn on details such as paper stock, binding methods, or publication frequency? It makes more sense to examine a medium's substance, its context, and especially its implications of veracity.

FIRST OF ALL, WHAT IS A PHOTOGRAPH?

As quoted in Chapter 3, one professional said: "I don't consider a photograph to be a photograph anymore. It's something to work with." Indeed, once a photo's elements have been fragmented, recolored, repositioned, and combined with elements from other photos or even other media altogether, is it still a "photograph"?

Here, the short answer is yes. If a published image is photo-based, looks like a photo, and contains no clear visual clues that it has been manipulated (recast as a photo-montage, for example), we will treat it as a photograph if for no other reason than the public is likely to do the same; in fact, we will treat it as a photograph for *precisely* that reason. (*Note*: In its photography alteration protocol, *National Geographic* defines photography as "any image captured through the use of an optical lens device and stored on any chemical, optical or electronic media.")

PHOTOJOURNALISM: EYEWITNESS TO HISTORY

No one argues that journalistic principles should apply to visual fiction invented for comic or fantastic effect. After all, readers do not expect the same correspondence to reality from an image of a 200-foot-tall beer bottle in a magazine advertisement and a front-page photo in *The Washington Post*. But what about the vast middle ground in between these extremes? How do we sort out tricky questions such as whether identical standards should apply to news magazines versus general interest magazines; "features" versus "articles"; magazine covers versus interior photos; or print versus online media?

Let us start with the kind of photography for which we might expect the strictest standards of all: photojournalism. Conventional definitions of "photojournalism," like those of journalism itself, are typically tied to the dissemination of news. The word often evokes the kind of photography enshrined for decades in *National Geographic* and *Life*. It is thought to provide a window on the world, an "eyewitness to history," as Peter Arnett wrote in *Flash! The Associated Press Covers the World*.[3] In the public mind, photojournalism is slice-of-life documentation, charged with a you-are-there immediacy and weighty with journalistic authority. In short, it is serious business.

Arnett asserts that "one of the stanchions of American democracy" is the notion that photojournalism provides viewers with "a firm basis of facts by which to form their own judgment." He adds, "If democracy is the voice of the people, then the AP is its stenographer." This stenographic or reportorial aspect of Associated Press photographers and other professionals is at the heart of our notions of photojournalism. We admire its practitioners for their competence, their persistence, their recognition of what is compelling or newsworthy, and sometimes their bravery. Their work may shed new light on a subject, or change our perceptions of society or nature. It may even rise to the level of art, but in any case it does not mislead. Photojournalistic images may be harrowing or soothing, extraordinary or mundane, artful or appalling, but above all they are, in a word, real.

Let us not dwell on the philosophical question of the ages: What is real? As we saw in Chapter 1, private citizens and media professionals alike regularly use the words "real" and "reality" in drawing ethical distinctions in visual media. Throughout this book we explore photography's objectivity, or lack of it. For now, let us simply acknowledge that photojournalism, as its name makes obvious, is a kind of journalism.

DO WE STILL KNOW WHAT JOURNALISM IS?

The problem is that "journalism" itself is so vaguely defined. If anything, its parameters are blurrier than ever, given the news media's adoption of entertainment values, the much-discussed convergence of media technologies,

FIGURE 10.1   More than a decade after the <u>St. Louis Post-Dispatch</u> removed a soda can from this news photo, professionals still debate the ethics of the decision. Says the paper's Larry Coyne: "It was a mistake; it would never happen here again."

and the blending of previously discrete practices or disciplines. One example: *The New York Times* in 1998 referred to "one of the hottest fashions in the media industry: the melding of journalism and Hollywood."[4] Several major magazines have sold stories to movie makers. For example, *Vanity Fair* writer Marie Brenner's article on a tobacco industry whistle blower was optioned by Disney. Brenner admitted that the Hollywood connection might affect content: "Are you doing an article because it might sell, or because it is journalistically sound?"[5]

Another vague distinction is the line between drama and documentary. The ostensibly nonfiction television programs *20/20, Unsolved Mysteries, America's Most Wanted, Saturday Evening with Connie Chung*, and *A Current Affair* have all mixed actual news footage with staged re-enactments.[6]

To appreciate how many barriers have been breached, consider all the hybrid terms and concepts entering the lexicon in recent years: *advertorial, infomercial, infotainment, docudrama, net 'zines*, "reality-based" entertainment, "magazine"-format television shows, and so on. Consider also how

FIGURE 10.1. Altered version

the Internet has allowed independent groups or even individuals to appropriate news-dissemination functions that once were the province of licensed stations and corporate networks.

The Disappearing Coke Can

One reflection upon the word "journalism" occurred in the aftermath of an altered photo published in the *St. Louis Post-Dispatch*; ironically, it pictured the 1989 Pulitzer Prize winner in news photography. The image of a Diet Coke can was optically removed from within the frame, as opposed to being cropped out (Figure 10.1). In a PBS video, Bill Moyers referred to the altered photo and asked, "Is this journalism?"[7]

Re-Examining the Term "Feature"

What is or is not journalism depends in part upon whom you ask, for "journalism" means different things to different people—and even to different journalists. Tina Brown, the editor of *Talk* magazine and former editor of

> Pictures taken of Jews before the war, photos of everyday life and family portraits, underwent a huge transformation. After the war, they wound up taking on the monumental significance of documenting the loss of a culture.
> —Jewish studies professor Jeffrey Shandler[8]

The New Yorker and *Vanity Fair*, said she would not digitally alter a photograph in a "journalism piece," but she has approved the substantial manipulation of other types of editorial photographs.[9] We might describe some of the articles in Ms. Brown's publications as "celebrity" journalism or "personality" journalism, but her comment suggests that in her view some of them are not journalism at all.

Tina Brown is not the only professional to subdivide his or her work into categories with different standards for photo alteration. Some have suggested different rules for "feature" sections and "news" sections in newspapers.[10] But how many newspapers locate all their "features" in separate sections? Do readers know or care about such distinctions? How many readers distinguish a "feature" from an "article" or "story"? Does it make any sense for some professionals to continue to associate the term "feature" with the rescued-kitty notion of "soft news," when for years the feature format has provided the ideal structure for some of journalism's most profound and hardest-hitting stories?

Beyond "Hard News"

If we are to preserve photography as a mass medium for conveying information about actual events, the natural world, and the experiences and emotions of real people, we must do better than falling back on old concepts of hard news. The distinctions professionals make between "soft features" and "hard news" are less important than public perceptions. Photocredibility doesn't depend on how professionals define their terms, but rather on whether readers believe they are being bamboozled. If readers bring an expectation of veracity to *any* photo appearing in a purportedly nonfiction environment, and the image turns out to have been staged or otherwise faked, credibility will surely decline in the publication and perhaps in visual journalism itself.

This is not to suggest that photographers apply the same rules to crime scenes and class reunions; as we saw in Chapter 7, readers allow and even expect a certain amount of posing in some cases. They may also accept manipulations to an obviously posed photo whose context from the first suggests only moderate authenticity.

But professionals should recognize the risks of publishing any purportedly nonfiction photo that does not mean what it appears to say (that is, a photo that does not meet its implication of authenticity), whether we call it

In his May 1998 <u>Atlantic Monthly</u> article, "Photography in the Age of Falsification," Kenneth Brower responded to a quote from wildlife photographer Art Wolfe.

Wolfe: "I often had to pass over photographs because in a picture of masses of animals invariably one would be wandering in the wrong direction, thereby disrupting the pattern I was trying to achieve. Today the ability to digitally alter this disruption is at hand."

Brower: "Wandering in the wrong direction according to whom? Whose patterns is the nature photographer supposed to celebrate — nature's or his own? In the human herd that animal wandering in the wrong direction would be the Buddha, or Luther, or Einstein."[11]

hard or soft, news or feature, and whether we fictionalize it by staging, cropping, airbrushing, digital manipulation, or other means.

THE "NONFICTION PHOTOGRAPHIC ENVIRONMENT": A PROPOSED DEFINITION

In laying a foundation for a method by which the ethics of an altered photo can be evaluated, this book generally avoids the terms "photojournalism" and "hard news," employing instead the more expansive "nonfiction photographic environment." Simply put, the term identifies a publishing context to which reasonable readers bring an expectation of veracity. That is, "nonfiction photographic environment" indicates *a mass-media context that presents photos taken for news, editorial, documentary, or other nonfiction purposes.*

Not merely semantic, this distinction between a "nonfiction photographic environment" and "photojournalism" is necessitated by the latter's traditional "hard news" connotation. Granted, altered images of battlefields, crime scenes, political events, and so on may be the most egregious examples of visual deception, but as we have seen throughout earlier chapters, manipulations to images *other* than hard news photos have already undermined faith in mass-media photography of all types. Thus "photojournalism" is too narrow to describe the category to which ethical standards should apply.

For our discussion, a "nonfiction photographic environment" embraces all newspaper, magazine, broadcast, cable, or online still photography that accompanies nonfiction text published or otherwise distributed in the mass media, including spontaneous glimpse-and-snap pictures as well as photos that are posed, arranged, and taken in studios or under other controlled conditions (some exceptions are listed below). Aside from photos that

> Should covers be held to a different standard than interior photos? No.
>
> — Deni Elliott, University of Montana[12]

accompany text, the definition also includes purportedly nonfiction, mass-media photos appearing alone, or in collections or photo essays. It includes images appearing in "general interest" as well as "hard news" publications, whether alongside news reports, so-called soft features, analyses, columns, or departments.

Let us recognize that within this category of nonfiction photography, images carry different levels of implied authenticity based upon context: a cooking magazine cover picturing an elegant dessert versus a newspaper photo of a street demonstration, for example. Suggestions and details follow.

Nature Photography

In a May 1998 *Atlantic Monthly* article, Kenneth Brower cited a June 1996 letter from photographer Gary Braasch to the North American Nature Photography Association's ethics committee. "Nature photographs are generally accepted as and trusted to be straightforward records of what the photographer witnessed and recorded on film in a single instant," Braasch wrote. "This is an acceptance hallowed by years of communication among photographers, editors, publishers, and viewers."[13]

But even nature photography's rules are ambiguous when it comes to manipulation. As Brower pointed out: "The fact is that this acceptance has often been 'hallowed' in the breach. As the advocates of digital doctoring like to point out, the old boys faked it too," sometimes rearranging scenes or posing subjects. (The Grand Prize Winner in *Alaska* magazine's 1996 photo contest was an acknowledged composite; the bear and the clouds were photographed on different days.)

Nonetheless, photography that purports to capture "nature" carries an implied promise of veracity and is therefore included in our definition of nonfiction photography. No distinction is made here between nature photography and "wildlife" photography, which, after all, promises that it reflects life in the wild rather than life in the zoo or life on the game preserve.

Magazine Covers

This book does not assert that we should hold all magazine covers to photojournalistic standards, only that we should not automatically exclude them from our discussion. A story titled "Kids for Sale," in the Sunday newspaper supplement *Parade*, addressed teenage prostitution. One of the three cover photos was taken by Pulitzer-Prize winner Eddie Adams; it pictured a paid model rather than an actual prostitute. Adams later explained that photos of underage subjects require the use of models because of the difficulty of gaining permission from parents.[14] While all working photographers can appreciate such obstacles, a simple note identifying the subject as a paid model could have avoided the ensuing controversy about the truthfulness of the photo.

In a September 1986 *News Photographer* article about the incident, Adams was quoted as saying that magazines set up cover pictures "to draw attention to the story, to illustrate a point. Newspapers have even more instances . . . with set-up feature pictures."[15] While magazine covers are indeed essential to newsstand success and are thus sales tools, consumers perceive them as being a showcase of sorts, a window into the magazine's interior, a promise of what's inside. For these reasons, covers are included in our definition.

In fact, as cited in Chapter 4, the most vehement objections to manipulated photography have been provoked not by hard-news photos in newspapers but by magazine covers, such as *National Geographic*'s relocated pyramid, *Time*'s "sinister" O.J. Simpson, and *Newsweek*'s orthodontically enhanced septuplet mom, Mrs. McCaughey. In those cases and others, readers rejected the argument that a cover's marketing function relieves it of its implication of authenticity. In each case, readers disapproved of the alterations, critics howled, and the magazines acknowledged their mistakes and apologized.

Visual journalists know better than anyone that images are often more powerful than words. (What do we remember of *Time* magazine's coverage of the O.J. Simpson trial? The cover stories that took hours to read? Or the June 27, 1994, cover image we glimpsed in a second?) Instead of tolerating lower standards because of a cover's acknowledged marketing function, perhaps we should recognize other factors that warrant *high* standards:

- A cover is the most conspicuous page of any magazine; its power and prominence only increase its potential for misleading viewers.
- A mismatch in authenticity between a magazine's cover and its contents seems to be a kind of false advertising.
- A cover is viewed not only by buyers of the magazine but also by passersby who may absorb the cover's message.

The question is not so much whether all magazine covers should be subject to one list of rigid rules, as opposed to another list for interior magazine photos and yet another for newspaper photos. Rather, given the function and the context of a cover image—or any image—what is its implication of authenticity? Does it meet that standard? Does it mean what it says?

Photojournalistic Book Covers

Some books have covers that do not literally reflect their contents, such as a math textbook with a cover picturing a work of fine art. There's nothing unethical about them. But cover imagery that misleads readers about the book's contents *is* unethical. As we learned in Chapter 5, the cover of

A Day in the Life of America: Photographed by 200 of the World's Leading Photojournalists on One Day was substantially manipulated (Figure 5.2). The photo director argued that covers are "advertising"—their primary function is to sell the book. True enough. In this case, however, the cover type promises that the book presents the work of "photojournalists." Anyone examining a book of unmanipulated photography would likely expect its cover photography to exemplify the contents and be unmanipulated as well. Thus the cover's *non*photojournalistic alterations might seem dubious, at least to some observers.

As with magazine covers, the point here is not that all book covers should be held to strict photojournalistic standards, but rather that along with their marketing functions they may carry some level of implied veracity, depending on accompanying text and other aspects of context. These implications affect whether manipulated cover images are ethical.

Nonfiction Television

During a New Year's Eve, 1999, broadcast covering festivities in Times Square, CBS News kicked off the new millennium by superimposing its digitally created logo over a sign sponsored by rival NBC. CBS anchor Dan Rather called the manipulation a mistake and admitted, "There is no excuse for it. At the very least we should have pointed out to viewers that we were doing it." Andrew Heyward, the president of CBS News, said, "We are not in the deception business; we're in the reality business," and yet he defended such manipulations, particularly on network programs such as *The Early Show*. According to Mr. Heyward, the technology provided "a whimsical and creative way to display our logo in various and unlikely places."

While such shows may not be "hard news," they are nevertheless purportedly nonfiction. Every time broadcasters use manipulated images that violate the expectations of their viewers, they are teaching those viewers not to trust what they see—and very likely not to trust what they hear or read. Given that journalism's credibility is already on the ropes, professionals should be doing everything they can to regain public trust rather than squandering what little trust remains.

The Fashion/Beauty Exclusion

One of the slipperiest of all categories is fashion/beauty magazines, in part because their mix of text and graphics is so odd. The articles supposedly promote self-discovery, self-awareness, and self-fulfillment, yet they are often accompanied by images that look not to the self at all, but rather to others, for standards of acceptance. The photos seem to say that you *should* look a certain way, but unless you are athletic or borderline anorexic, you don't and probably never will.

These publications disseminate health news, makeup tips, weight-loss "secrets," and other purportedly factual information with breathless enthusiasm, and many critics believe they affect readers' self-esteem in meaningful ways. But at the same time, much of what passes for editorial is virtual advertising material, and advertisers dictate editorial policy to an extent that would appall editors in other fields.[16] In fashion, drastically manipulated photography is taken for granted by art directors and editors (if not necessarily by readers), and editorial layouts are sometimes barely distinguishable from advertising spreads.

For all these reasons, fashion/beauty publications are deemed so atypical as to warrant excluding them from this discussion. Still, the manufacturing of mass-media "beauty" images is both fascinating and significant, as evidenced by the many books, articles and scholarly papers that have addressed the topic.[17] For our purposes here, please see the discussion in Chapter 17 regarding "cosmetic" retouching.

Other Exclusions

The proposed definition of the nonfiction photographic environment excludes photos obviously created as stand-alone artworks, even if they accompany journalistic text, as well as marketing, public relations, promotional and advertising photography, unless such work is represented to the public as being unmanipulated or "real." (The alteration of photography in advertising and in fashion/beauty editorial is certainly worth discussing; however, it is simply outside the scope of this book.) The definition also excludes photos taken and used for personal purposes—wedding photos, family portraits, and the like.

SUMMARY

The strictest definitions of photojournalism and hard news are too narrow to describe photography that should be held to reasonable ethical standards, for the simple reason that mass-media audiences do not confine their expectations of veracity to photojournalism or to hard news. If anything, public outcries against manipulated photography have proved the opposite. Time and again, readers and media professionals alike have condemned manipulated photos of many types—sports, human interest, local news, photo ops, nature, landscape, in newspapers, on magazine covers, on book covers, and so on (for a list of examples, see Chapter 4).

As proposed here, "nonfiction photographic environments" include newspaper, magazine, newsletter, book, or online nonfiction mass-media contexts, from hard news to general interest features, from covers to interior photos. The concept embraces, but is significantly broader than, some conceptions of photojournalism and hard news. It recognizes within these environments a range or spectrum of implied authenticity. It excludes obvious artistic creations (surreal photo-fantasies, for example), photos used for personal purposes, and images used in fiction, advertising, and fashion/beauty editorial. The concept can be extended to broadcast, online, cable, and video documentary journalism.

Defining the nonfiction photographic environment is only a preliminary step in assessing altered photos. We will discover that even within that category, many factors can affect whether images are perceived to be real or fictional, ethical or unethical.

EXPLORATIONS

1. Different ethical codes have evolved for different media—television, nonfiction books and so on, or even for different subsections within a single medium (hard news vs. features, in some cases). In recent years, however, previously distinct media have merged in different ways. An online "publication" may mix elements of newsletters, newspapers, and magazines along with digital resources—indexes, archival material, links to other publications, even audio and video. Given the fact that in the digital realm, lines between books, magazines, pamphlets, catalogs, and the like are indistinct, how can we update categories of nonfiction media so as to evaluate an image's ethics? To what general principles can we turn? Among various media, what distinguishing characteristics might raise or lower their ethical standards?

2. What do you think of the rationalizations offered above in defense of manipulating the cover of *A Day in the Life of America* (Figure 5.2)? Would typical readers accept the notion that photojournalistic book covers have ethical standards less stringent than the contents of the very books they advertise? Would readers extend the notion to, say, magazine covers? If so, how could we explain the negative public reaction and the publishers' apologies following *Time*'s darkened and blurred O.J. Simpson cover, *Newsweek*'s digital-dentistry cover, or *National Geographic*'s relocated pyramid cover?

3. Regarding *A Day in the Life of America: Photographed by 200 of the World's Leading Photojournalists on One Day*, compare the implications of the title and subtitle to Tim Fitzharris's *Virtual Wilderness: The Nature Photographer's Guide to Computer Imaging*.

4. The cover story of the March 1996 *Men's Journal* was "Spring Fever! 22 Totally New Adventures." The cover photo pictures an ocean background and a swimsuited couple wading through shallow water in the foreground (Figure 10.2). In this rear-view photo, the woman perches atop the man's shoulders; both carry snorkeling gear. Computer retouching removed the woman's bathing suit top; presumably, it was decided her bare back would render the cover sexier and more commercial.

   Briefly review the "Diet Coke" example and the *Newsweek* cover of Mrs. McCaughey, both discussed in this chapter. How does the *Men's Journal* cover compare to those alterations? Compare the

FIGURE 10.2.   Considering the magazine, the subject of the story, and the image it-self, what is the implied level of authenticity of this photo? Would it surprise anyone to learn that these people are models, or that the scene was arranged by the photographer?

publications, the functions of their photographs, and their levels of implied authenticity. Do these differences affect the ethics of the photo alterations?

5. Although not a digitally manipulated photo, *Time*'s cover of April 4, 1994 raises the issue of implied authenticity (Figure 10.3). The cover type: "Deep Water: How the president's men tried to hinder the Whitewater investigation." The caption appearing on the cover: "White House Senior Adviser George Stephanopoulos with

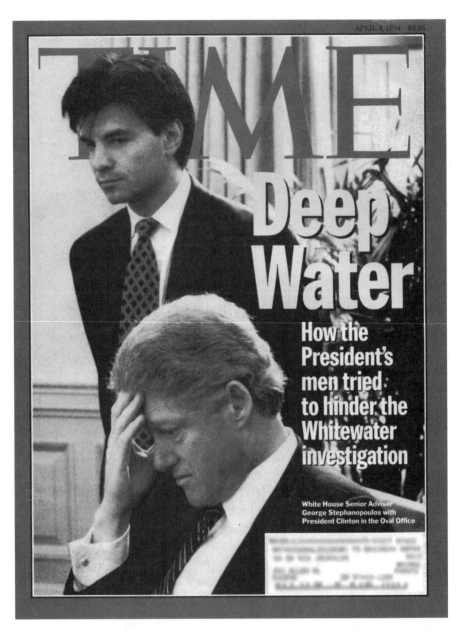

FIGURE 10.3.   Considering the magazine, the cover type, and the image itself, what is this photo's implication of authenticity? How does it compare to that of the Men's Journal "Spring Fever!" cover?

President Clinton in the Oval Office." In the photo both men look grim; the president's head is lowered; he has one hand on his forehead. As it turns out, the image had been taken during a scheduling meeting the previous year and had nothing to do with Whitewater. Many readers protested, but *Time* defended the photo, which "more than any other we had in our files, represented the close working relationship between these two men. We chose it not to mislead readers but to convey a mood. ... The use of this photograph, with no date, conformed to our usual practice."[18]

Given the context—the cover of a weekly news magazine— would the combination of cover type, caption and photo suggest the photo had been taken during the crisis in question? Discuss where such photos lie along the spectrum of implied authenticity; contrast the *Time* "Deep Water" and *Men's Journal* "Spring Fever!" covers.

6. *USA Today* ran a story about street violence. A photo depicted several gun-wielding Los Angeles gang members, some of whom later complained that they had been told that the story concerned a program in which gun owners could trade in their weapons for job opportunities. *USA Today* admitted the photo was "misleading."[19] Discuss the relationship between the actual photo and its implications of authenticity.

ENDNOTES

1. Alex MacLeod is the managing editor of the *Seattle Times, Associated Press*, March 31, 1997.
2. Attempts to categorize mass-media images in terms of their authenticity are not new. In 1929, photographer Robert Miller suggested that newspaper photography could be divided into "news photography" and "pictorial journalism." The latter entailed more artistry and fewer restraints. Robert R. Miller, "News-Photography versus Pictorial Journalism," *Photo-Era* 63 (October 1929).
3. Peter Arnett, *Flash! The Associated Press Covers the World* (New York: Abrams, 1998).
4. James Sterngold, "Journalism Goes Hollywood, and Hollywood Is Reading," *The New York Times* (July 10, 1998): C5.
5. Nicholas Stein, "Hollywood Two-Step: The Risky Dance of Editors and Agents," *Columbia Journalism Review* (November/December 1998): http://www.cjr.org/year/98/6/hollywood.asp.
6. Paul Lester, *Photojournalism: An Ethical Approach* (Hillsdale, NJ: Lawrence Erlbaum Assoc., 1991), 128.
7. "Consuming Images," *The Public Mind: Image and Reality in America* (PBS video, 1989). See also, S. Kramer, "The Case of the Missing Coke Can: Electronically Altered Photo Creates a Stir," *Editor & Publisher* (April 29, 1989): 18–19; E. Rogers, "Now You See It, Now You Don't: Coke Can's Disappearance Spotlights Potential for Editing Abuse," *News Photographer* (August 1989): 16.
8. Dan Gilgoff, "Gone but Never Forgotten," *U.S. News & World Report* (July 9–16, 2001): 44.
9. Brown was the editor of *Vanity Fair* when she was quoted. Jonathan Alter, "When Photographs Lie," *Newsweek* (July 30, 1990): 45.
10. Shiela Reaves, "Magazines vs. Newspapers: Editors Have Different Ethical Standards on The Digital Manipulation of Photographs," *Visual Communications Quarterly* 2, no. 1 (winter 1995): 4. "Newspaper editors are intolerant of altering spot news photos and much more tolerant of altering photo illustrations, and they have mixed reactions to altering feature photos." Reaves, "The Vulnerable Image: Categorization of Photo Types as Predictor of Digital Manipulation," a paper presented to the Visual Communication Division, AEJMC annual convention, August 1992. See also, Reaves, "Digital Alteration of Photographs in Magazines: An Examination of the Ethics," *Journal of Mass Media Ethics*, no. 3 (1991): 175.
11. Brower, 108–9.
12. From an e-mail correspondence with the author, fall 1998.
13. Kenneth Brower, "Photography in the Age of Falsification," *Atlantic Monthly* (May 1998): 95.
14. Lester, *Photojournalism*, 120.

15. B. Brill, "Town Protests Staged Picture, 'Hooker Image,' " *News Photographer* (September 1986): 4–8.

16. For example, see Gloria Steinem, "Sex, Lies & Advertising," *Ms.* (July/August 1990): 18–25.

17. For example, see Naomi Wolf, *The Beauty Myth: How Images of Beauty Are Used against Women* (New York: Morrow, 1991); Margaret Finders, "Queens and Teen Zines: Adolescent Females Reading Their Way toward Adulthood," *Anthropology and Education Quarterly* 27 (1996): 71–89.

18. "Undated Cover Picture," Letters, *Time* (April 25, 1994): 11.

19. G. Bruce Knecht, "At *USA Today*, a Staged Photo Isn't Good News," *Wall Street Journal* (August 22, 1996): B7.

Chapter 11

Introducing the Reader's "Qualified Expectation of Reality"
The Quote Standard

Photography and the public have an unusual compact. "The camera does not lie" is a proposition that most of us know to be false yet we half believe anyway.

—Kenneth Brower[1]

LOOKING BEYOND THE "ALTERED CONTENT" DISTINCTION

Chapter 10 described nonfiction images that carry varying levels of implied authenticity and therefore should be held to reasonable ethical standards. But what are reasonable standards, exactly? Earlier chapters described ethical photos as those that conform to their implied authenticity: They reflect or correspond to reality in the manner in which reasonable viewers would expect them to, given their subject matter, context and so on. They mean what they say.

We have also seen that readers and professionals alike use descriptions such as "real" and "a picture of reality" when distinguishing these legitimate nonfiction photos from unethical manipulations. In fact, across the spectrum of discussion—in textbooks, readers' letters to editors, professionals' critiques, codes of ethics, surveys, photo contest rules—the one constant is a conviction that journalistic photos must reflect reality. We may assume, then, that such photos are rendered unethical when their relationship to reality is disrupted. Somewhere between improving the contrast in a man's face and replacing his face with that of someone else, a line is crossed. But where?

In answering the question, it is not helpful to assign an ethical hierarchy to various techniques. Whether the effect is achieved with scissors, airbrushing, or software is less relevant than whether it is misleading. We have also recognized earlier in this book the inadequacy of basing ethical standards solely upon the publication's categorization as a magazine, newspaper, newsletter, and so on, or an article's description as "hard news" or a "soft feature."

As we saw in Chapter 8, many analyses and codes draw a line between altering a photo's content and enhancing what's already there. But by itself, even this crucial distinction sometimes falls short as a benchmark of photo-truth. After all, cropping a photo could be far more misleading than digitally rearranging its content if the crop were applied to material elements, the rearrangement to unnoticed details.

To better grasp perceived reality in journalistic imagery, this chapter examines an analogy: perceived reality in journalistic text.

THE QUOTE STANDARD

It is useful to compare assumptions about visual information within the frame of a photograph to assumptions about statements "framed" by quotation marks. Although quote marks suggest that the words appear in print precisely as spoken, in fact quotes are sometimes altered by journalists, even responsible ones. The appropriateness of this practice has long been debated (and occasionally litigated), and an evolving spectrum of opinion reflects journalists' differing approaches.

Of course, the standards of some journalists are higher than others, but even professionals who strive to be ethical can simply disagree as to whether a quote can be altered, and how (or if) such alterations should be disclosed. Variables may include the publication's mission, the speaker's status, and the perceived aesthetic drawbacks of brackets, ellipses, editor's notes, and other indicators or labels.

When a newspaper reports a diplomat's press conference, for example, quoted material might well be considered untouchable, with every omission indicated by ellipses, every addition by brackets. Yet over the years even highly respected, big-city dailies such as *The Washington Post* and *The New York Times* have differed in regard to the necessity of using ellipses and brackets to indicate every alteration, and even staunch advocates of the "purist" approach sometimes allow for "cleaning up" the grammar or removing "ums" and "uhs."[2]

> Similar to a direct quote from a person, documentary photographs are seen as visual direct quotes from reality, by which we can be sure of the previous existence of the things in front of the camera. . . . digital imaging alterations penetrate into the inner structure of an image and change a direct quote to an indirect quote or even a distorted quote. . . . Digitization destroys the fixity of a photograph . . . making truth about reality unstable and shifting.
>
> — Edgar Huang[3]

Journalists who consider themselves purists might also allow for other types of alterations, so long as readers are presumed to take them for granted or are informed of them. An obscene word might be replaced with its first letter and hyphens, for example, or a composite interview might be allowed if accompanied by an explanatory note from the editor.

Editorial text other than what journalists call "hard news" often entails a more lenient approach. Readers probably would not be stunned to learn that some interviews in entertainment magazines, although considered nonfiction, are nevertheless composites of conversations and follow-up talks conducted on several occasions, or that quoted comments are sometimes smoothed, spliced, or otherwise edited to account for gestures invisible to readers, or to improve clarity, or to remove redundancies, irrelevancies, and interruptions.

In summary, enlightened policies attempt to reconcile conflicting yet reasonable points of view. On the one hand, it is only sensible to recognize that when readers see statements in quote marks, they imagine hearing the speaker say them precisely as reported. On the other hand, it is just as sensible to concede that the spoken language differs from the written one, that something happens when words are removed from their context and committed to print. Even the strictest purists recognize that ethical practice sometimes goes beyond merely reporting verbatim recitations; after all, if taken out of context, verbatim quotes can distort the intent of what was said and do a disservice to the subject and readers alike. The same can be said of "verbatim" (unmanipulated) photos when published in unrepresentative or otherwise misleading contexts.

THE READER'S "QUALIFIED EXPECTATION OF REALITY"

Thoughtful journalists recognize that when encountering quotes, readers bring a certain *expectation of reality* to the page, an assumption that words set off in quote marks were actually uttered by the speaker. As revealed by their techniques and practices, however, most journalists also believe that

> There is a new visual literacy. . . . It's like verbal literacy. I'm thinking of the New Journalism: Tom Wolfe came along and did stories that caused an uproar because he was using events based in truth, but manipulating them. We're thinking about whether these images are true or real, but look at the text that goes beside them: How much manipulation is done there reflecting the point of view of the journalist or editor? Now photography and images are starting to pose the same questions.
>
> — Rhonda Rubenstein, designer and teacher[4]

If we look at the issue of extracting parts of an image and recombining them, nobody would object if I said, "Gee, that's a great red pixel. I'm going to pull that red pixel out and use it." That's an extreme case. Then, step by step, you quote larger and larger pieces, until at some point — it's not very clearly definable — you get to the point where you're quoting and recombining in ways you don't usually think of. In text, that's been fairly well covered. I think we'll see the same kinds of expectations developing with digital images.

—William J. Mitchell, MIT[5]

this expectation may be *qualified* by allowances for accommodating the shift in context from the in-person interview to its published report, and further qualified by recognizing differences between written and spoken versions of the language. Such allowances might permit the correction of grammar, the elimination of clutter or, in some cases, judicious splicing and smoothing.

But all across the spectrum of opinion, one principle stands inviolate: No matter where the journalist draws the line on details such as the use of ellipses or brackets, readers' expectations invariably demand the preservation of the speaker's fundamental meaning. We can adopt this principle when processing visual information. In fact, a commitment to avoiding deception has guided professionals in the darkroom for decades and will serve us well as we grapple with issues of digital technology—provided we apply it consistently, publicize it, and stick to it.

Responsible policies toward presenting journalistic quotes may be summarized by the following points, each of which has a direct corollary in visual journalism:

- Ethical professionals may disagree as to whether or how a quote can be altered.
- Ethical professionals may disagree as to how (or if) alterations should be revealed to readers.
- Even self-styled purists sometimes allow for "cleaning up" the grammar.
- Policies may vary according to the circumstances under which a quote is uttered or the publishing environment in which it appears.
- "Hard news" may have stricter standards than other categories that are nevertheless journalistic and that carry at least some implications of veracity.
- Ethical practice sometimes goes beyond reporting verbatim recitations, which can distort meaning if taken out of context.

> In the aftermath of <u>Time</u>'s O.J. Simpson cover, <u>Newsweek</u> assistant managing editor Mark Whitaker compared journalistic photography to journalistic text: "Once it ceases to be real, it is as if you were making up a story."[6]

- Enlightened policies attempt to reconcile conflicting yet reasonable points of view.
- Regardless of technical policy differences among publications, all responsible journalists agree that maintaining the quote's meaning is essential.

SUMMARY

Like journalistic writers and their readers, visual journalists and their viewers share a set of assumptions that provides the foundation for photography's long-lived credibility. This "Qualified Expectation of Reality,"[7] or QER, derives from professional codes of ethics, the traditions of photographic grammar, some presumed public awareness of rudimentary photographic processes, and a public faith founded on decades of experience.

In journalistic features as well as hard news, photos are similar to quotes in one respect: Their responsible processing accommodates readers' expectations of reality, as reasonably qualified. In the text of feature stories, readers allow for shifts in structure and sometimes a level of subjectivity unacceptable in "inverted pyramid" articles or hard news accounts. Nevertheless, journalistic feature articles must meet their implications of authenticity; they may not be fictionalized. Similarly, journalistic feature *photos* should be held to the same standard. Continuing our focus on the readers' expectation of reality, the next chapter defines "photofiction."

EXPLORATIONS

1. Bring to class examples from newspapers or magazines in which a journalist has quoted someone and disclosed an alteration to the quote. Look for the use of brackets, ellipses (…), notations such as "emphasis added," and the like. In each case, consider (a) where the quote appears, (b) the role or status of the speaker or writer being quoted, and (c) the nature of the "disclosure." How do these three elements relate to each other?

2. Suppose you tape-record an interview and transcribe it in exact detail. What sorts of alterations to quotes, if any, would you be willing to make in converting your verbatim transcript into a publishable

article for a daily newspaper? Arrange the categories of alterations progressing from minor to major. What sorts of alterations would *not* be appropriate? Can you state a guideline or principle that separates inappropriate from appropriate alterations?

3. Regarding the previous question, would your answers vary with different types of publications? If so, how?

4. Repeat the exercise from questions 2 and 3, this time addressing photographic negatives rather than a transcription of quotes.

5. Chapter 6 mentioned the "marketplace of ideas," as advocated by Mill in *On Liberty*: In order for a free people to make appropriate decisions about their own lives and their governments, they must be exposed to the broadest possible range of ideas and have the ability to openly debate such ideas and to express themselves to their fellow citizens. Consider the extent to which nonfiction mass-media images form our impressions of our world and sometimes help frame our public discussions of politics and social and economic issues. Discuss the qualified expectation of reality that readers bring to those images. Then discuss the relevance of photo manipulation to Mill's marketplace of ideas.

ENDNOTES

1. Kenneth Brower, "Photography in the Age of Falsification," *Atlantic Monthly* (May 1998): 109.
2. For example, see Brooks, Kennedy, Moen, and Ranly, "Problems in Direct Quotation," *News Reporting and Writing*, 4th ed. (New York: St. Martin's, 1992), 123–31.
3. Edgar Shaohua Huang, "Readers' Perception of Digital Alteration and Truth-Value in Documentary Photographs," submitted in partial fulfillment for a Ph.D. degree, School of Journalism, Indiana University (October 1999), 26–27.
4. Rhonda Rubenstein is an art director, magazine designer, CD-ROM developer, and teacher. Janet Abrams, "Little Photoshop of Horrors: The Ethics of Manipulating Journalistic Imagery," *Print* (November/December 1995): 28.
5. Professor Mitchell is the dean of the School of Architecture and Planning at MIT and author of *The Reconfigured Eye: Visual Truth in the Post-Photographic Era*. Abrams, 44.
6. "Photo Flap: *Time*'s Altered Image Sparks Ethics Debate," *The Phoenix Gazette* (June 22, 1994): A2.
7. Tom Wheeler and Tim Gleason, "Digital Photography and the Ethics of Photofiction: Four Tests for Assessing the Reader's Qualified Expectation of Reality," paper presented at the annual convention of the Association for Education in Journalism and Mass Communication (AEJMC), Magazine Division, Atlanta, Georgia, 1994, 10–11.

Chapter 12

Previewing the Guidelines for Photo Assessment

Defining "Photofiction"

journalism (jûr_ne-lîz_em) noun
1. The collecting, writing, editing, and presentation of news or news articles in newspapers and magazines and in radio and television broadcasts.

fiction (fîk_shen) noun
1. An imaginative creation or a pretense that does not represent actuality but has been invented. . . .
2. A lie.

—*The American Heritage Dictionary*[1]

Chapters 10 and 11 laid groundwork by outlining the nonfiction photographic environment and the reader's Qualified Expectation of Reality (QER). Building upon those concepts, and taking into account aspects of photographic context, Chapters 12 through 16 define "photofiction" and provide tests to reveal examples of it, help distinguish obvious from hidden photofiction, and offer suggestions for disclosure. Underlying every step is the reader's QER.

DEFINING "POST-EXPOSURE PHOTOFICTION"

Astute readers know that a news report does not reflect the whole world, but only glimpses and interpretations of a tiny fraction of it. We recognize that journalists select relatively few stories from a deluge of incoming reports and leads, and that even those professionals who strive to be objective impart at least some degree of their own perspectives or points of view. Certainly, we criticize them when we perceive their accounts to be biased or inaccurate, yet we reserve a special term for an account of something that never happened at all. We call it fiction.

If professionals and consumers think of ethical nonfiction photography as "a picture of reality," we can use reality's opposite—fiction—in describing unethical alterations. We will use the term *post-exposure photofiction* to apply to a class of altered photos defined and limited by three requirements:[2]

1. *The manipulation occurs after the shutter is clicked, that is, during processing.* Of course, a purportedly journalistic photo that is deceptive is unethical, regardless of whether its misleading aspects were introduced before or after exposure. But for our limited purposes, this restriction generally directs our inquiry away from pre-exposure activities such as posing and staging, already exhaustively discussed in the literature of photography.

2. *Material elements within the frame are added, removed, substantially altered, or rearranged by one method or another.* Again, it's the result, not the technique, that determines whether a photo alteration is ethical, but this requirement helps to focus our discussion for the most part on manipulations facilitated by recent technologies, as opposed to cropping and other techniques within the established grammar of photography.

3. *The manipulation changes the photo's meaning.*

Although the first two requirements help distinguish a particular class of manipulation, we have mentioned other classes as well. As we have seen, photographs can mislead in different ways. A staged event can be made to look spontaneous. Or, prior to clicking the shutter, the photographer can rearrange elements within the frame to suggest a condition that isn't true. Similarly, he or she can later crop out a material element that, again, could suggest a condition that isn't true.

The ethics of staging and posing and the appropriateness of darkroom procedures such as cropping have been addressed in many texts, codes, and articles, and summarized in previous chapters of this book. Although our primary concern is post-exposure manipulation, particularly as accomplished through digital means, those long-running debates about posing, cropping, and so on enlighten us because they, too, address readers' qualified expectations of reality.

For some observers, photofiction's third criterion is redundant—in their view, *any* addition, removal, substantial alteration, or rearrangement of

---

History has witnessed a horrible episode in which the Chinese government's spokesman, Yuan Mu, impudently denied the fact that ordinary citizens were killed in the 1989 Tiananmen Massacre, as shown in the news photographs carried in the Western media. The underlying argument ... was that the veracity, or the witness function, of those news photographs in the [age] of digital imaging was questionable. In the future, governments may be less afraid of the documentary evidence of photography.

— Edgar Huang[3]

material elements within the frame *automatically* changes a photo's relationship to perceived reality, or its meaning—but for our purposes it is useful to discuss meaning as a separate consideration.

BEYOND EXISTING CODES

As we saw in Chapters 6 through 9, the bedrock of photojournalistic ethics is a commitment to truthfulness, reflected in proscriptions against altering content or otherwise deceiving the public. In applying this principle to new technologies, *National Geographic* editor Bill Allen wrote, "After a bumpy beginning, I believe that the magazine has the ethics of digital manipulation down right. . . . Do not alter reality on the finished image, except when it is done for some instructional purpose. And then make sure we tell our readers what was done, and why."[4]

National Geographic's policy could serve as an ideal starting point for all nonfiction visual communicators, and in some cases it could be applied without confusion or debate. In many other cases, however, more specific tests would help determine at what point "correcting" or "improving" or otherwise "processing" an image alters its reality.

Also helpful would be guidelines for answering such questions as the following:

- When is an example of photofiction so obvious that it will fool no one, and how might that status affect its ethics?
- When is a disclosure of an alteration necessary?
- How do we word such a disclosure?
- Where do we locate it?
- Is there a universal wording or symbol that will work in every case, or might different types of images, alterations, and publications require different disclosures?

PREVIEW: THE PHOTO-ASSESSMENT TESTS IN BRIEF

One of the more extensive explorations of photographic credibility in the "age of electronic simulation" is William Mitchell's *The Reconfigured Eye: Visual Truth in the Post-Photographic Era*.[5] The book suggests that the credibility of photography depends on preserving criteria that Mitchell characterized as adherence to the referent; intention and objectivity; technical coherence; and relationship to visual discourse.[6] In 1994, those criteria were applied in conceiving the following tests for assessing the ethics of an altered photo:

- the viewfinder test
- nonfiction photography's process test
- the technical credibility test
- the test of obvious implausibility[7]

Michael Sand asked the brilliant photographer and digital photo artist Pedro Meyer whether he would ever return to straight documentary photography. Meyer: "The question implies that I have left the straight documentary tradition, doesn't it? So let's first address the question of what can be considered 'straight.' I think that such a notion is, after all, only a convention determined by certain customs, technological limitations, and traditions. An ancient Egyptian or a Mixtec would probably not recognize photographs as constituting a 'straight documentary' representation. My work will also be seen as 'straight' by coming generations. We are in for some serious rethinking of photographic theories of representation, especially when it concerns the documentary tradition."

— Pedro Meyer, Truths & Fictions[8]

Addressed in upcoming chapters, these tests help reveal whether a photo meets the reader's QER. Of course, determining reader expectations is itself a judgment call, and professionals may disagree about a photo's implications of authenticity. In any case, a purportedly nonfiction image that violates or falls outside the reader's QER poses an ethical challenge, one that can usually be met with disclosure. A fifth test, the "essence of the image," helps determine appropriate disclosure.

A SET OF ADAPTABLE PRINCIPLES

The Qualified Expectation of Reality is a liberal standard. It recognizes varying levels of implied authenticity within nonfiction photographic environments, and it allows for conventional enhancements and processes such as routine cropping that do not mislead. It may even allow for photofiction—*if* readers are made aware of it, either because of its implausibility or by its labeling. Ultimately, the photojournalist must ask: Is the photo misleading?

Keep in mind that the proposed tests are not to be regarded as a comprehensive list of do's and don'ts. Despite the enviable simplicity of such lists, even the good ones are limited:

- Some apply only to a narrow class of publications or even to a single publication, and neither transfer well nor lend themselves to extrapolation.
- Some restrict themselves to the narrowest connotations of "photojournalism," ignoring other types of images that carry implied promises of veracity and thus affect media credibility.

> If professionals do their jobs with news photography, photo-journalism can weather the digital age. But they must nurture the reputation of being purists and curmudgeons, and of avoiding manipulation. . . . I would hope professionals would be equally vigilant to feature photos — the non-news, timeless photographs that involve candid moments and unposed serendipities. And I would hope these defenders of photo-journalism would keep portraits as real as the initial negative. Posing and coaching a subject for personal expression is fine, but leave it alone after the shutter snaps.
>
> —Shiela Reaves, University of Wisconsin[9]

- Some, by specifying one type of alteration (rearranging content, for example), may ignore other alterations that also can mislead viewers.
- Some, by specifying one technology (e.g., digital), may fail to address misleading alterations made with other processes.
- Some disallow photofictional illustrations that, if obviously fictional or if identified as fiction, could be ethical in appropriate contexts.

For all of these reasons, a more comprehensive and philosophically based approach is required. This approach accommodates a sufficiently broad class of images, various methods of alteration, different media, varying levels of sophistication among viewerships, and the dizzying speed with which media technologies and structures are evolving.

On the other hand, these guidelines are intended to be useful; if a publication uses them to adapt a practical, concrete, and credibility-preserving list of do's and don'ts, they will have served their purpose. Once a professional or student is familiar with these principles, applying them to an image often takes less than a minute.

Finally, these are suggested guidelines, not mathematical formulas or immutable laws of physics. As such, they are subject to interpretation. Decisions about altering photos come down to the individual's judgment about an image's implied authenticity, and about his her own responsibilities. In that regard, at least, nothing has changed since the invention of photography a century and a half ago.

SUMMARY

The three-element definition of post-exposure photofiction defines a broad class of alterations and also helps focus our attention on alterations rendered by digital technologies. Upcoming chapters provide flexible guidelines for implementing new technologies in ethical, credibility-preserving ways. These guidelines incorporate tests that may be applied quickly to any situation. As we will see, while the tests help to answer distinct questions, they work together and often overlap. An image may pass all of them, fail all of them, or pass some and fail others.

EXPLORATIONS

1. Bring to class examples of what you perceive to be "truthful" and "fictional" photographs in editorial (non-advertising) contexts in newspapers or magazines. What characteristics are typical of each type of photograph? Can you find examples of photographs that lie between the extremes of truth and fiction? What clues suggest that the images might be truthful, or might be fictional?

2. Have you ever worked on the graphics for your school newspaper or yearbook? What sorts of limitations, if any, have you placed on the alteration of photos?

3. For many photographers and viewers, the line between acceptable and unacceptable alteration is crossed when the photographer or processor goes beyond enhancement to altering content. But might radically manipulated imagery somehow be used to reveal reality and a larger truth, the way a fictional novel can?

    Acclaimed photographer and digital photo artist Pedro Meyer was asked about his computerized composites, photomontages, and other profoundly symbolic works: Given that his book *Truths & Fictions* is about "the creation of memories," was he in a sense fabricating experiences that did not occur? He replied, "I don't see it that way at all. All my images are about documenting experiences—not fabricating them. The experience in a traditional photographic representation has been limited (though in truth the camera sees more than we do, and therefore is not limited at all) to those elements that the lens was able to capture. To the silver halides or dyes, I now can add my own memory.

    "For example, the warplanes [which were added to] the image *Desert Shower* respond exactly to my memory; they actually did fly by. I just wasn't able to capture that on film. My limitation, the camera's, who cares? The fact is that what I see on the negative is not what happened in reality . . . with digital technology, I was able to restore the picture to my memory of what actually happened. Did I fabricate an experience in that case?"[10]

    What do you think? Is it possible to add, subtract, or rearrange material elements within a photo in order to re-create or reveal aspects of reality—without undermining public faith in visual journalism? What sort of disclosure would be required? Would it be necessary to separate such images from conventional contexts (newspapers, etc.), portraying them in other media such as books that resemble collections of artworks? Or could such images appear anywhere, provided their alterations were adequately disclosed?

ENDNOTES

1. *The American Heritage Dictionary of the English Language, Third Edition* is licensed from Houghton Mifflin. Copyright 1992 Houghton Mifflin. All rights reserved.
2. Tom Wheeler and Tim Gleason, "Digital Photography and the Ethics of Photofiction: Four Tests for Assessing the Reader's Qualified Expectation of Reality," paper presented at the annual convention of the Association for Education in Journalism and Mass Communication (AEJMC), Magazine Division, Atlanta, 1994.
3. Edgar Shaohua Huang, "Readers' Perception of Digital Alteration and Truth-Value in Documentary Photographs," submitted in partial fulfillment for a Ph.D. degree, School of Journalism, Indiana University (October 1999), 28. Dr. Huang cited Fred Ritchin, *In Our Own Image: The Coming Revolution in Photography: How Computer Technology Is Changing Our View of the World* (New York: Aperture, 1990, 1999), 5–7. Regarding photographic forgeries perpetrated by the Chinese government, see also "Bejing Double Take," *U.S. News and World Report* (March 28, 1988): 11.
4. From the editor, *National Geographic* (April 1998).
5. William J. Mitchell, *The Reconfigured Eye: Visual Truth in the Post-Photographic Era* (Cambridge: MIT Press, 1992).
6. Mitchell, 24–42.
7. Wheeler and Gleason, "Digital Photography," 7–10.
8. Pedro Meyer, *Truths & Fictions: A Journey from Documentary to Digital Photography* (New York: Aperture, 1995), 110.
9. Photojournalist Shiela Reaves is an associate professor at the School of Journalism and Mass Communication at the University of Wisconsin, Madison, and the author of many scholarly papers on retouching photos. From an e-mail correspondence with the author, fall 1998.
10. From an interview with Michael Sand, in Meyer, 109–10.

Chapter 13

Photofiction Tests 1 and 2

The Viewfinder and
Nonfiction Photography's Process Tests

Photographic darkrooms are quickly being replaced by computer workstation light-rooms. But as long as photojournalists do not subtract or add parts of a picture's internal elements, almost any other manipulation once accomplished in a photographic darkroom is considered ethical for news-editorial purposes.

—Paul Lester[1]

THE VIEWFINDER TEST IN NEWS PHOTOS

Viewers come to a journalistic photograph with the confidence that had they been standing next to the photographer at the scene, they would have witnessed the same "reality" found in the printed photo. That is, they expect the arrangement of scenes, objects, people and backgrounds to be no more or less than what the photographer saw through the viewfinder—with some allowances for routine processing.

While a photo's failure to pass this "viewfinder test" may reveal it to be photofiction, the test does not prohibit traditional processing or cropping, nor does it deny the interpretative nature of photography. It does, however, forbid the use of digital or other means to add material objects to a journalistic photograph, or to remove them, or to rearrange or substantially alter objects within it. Chapter 4 lists more than a dozen examples of manipulated nonfiction photography. A few were staged; all others failed the viewfinder test.

But It's Just a Tiny Detail . . .

Some would argue that adding, removing or rearranging a relatively unimportant object within the frame (for aesthetic reasons, let's say) is harmless, does not change the photo's meaning, and does not necessarily render the image fictional—despite technically violating the viewfinder test.

Is there hope for journalistic photography? Yes, we can expect news photos to mean the best depiction of external reality as possible. This "best depiction" standard gives photojournalists and their editors great latitude in the use of new technology. I would argue that it is OK to digitally retouch the sky in a photo of the [space shuttle] Challenger accident if the retouching creates a product that best depicts what one would see through the viewfinder. It is not OK to remove, add, or adjust perspective in a news photo because that is not the best depiction.

— Deni Elliott, University of Montana[2]

Then again, as previously mentioned, for some observers *any* addition, removal, substantial alteration, or rearranging of material elements *automatically* changes a photo's meaning by altering its relationship to perceived reality; this misleads viewers by violating their reasonable expectations, and renders the photo unethical in journalistic contexts.

While it may be enlightening to debate whether this or that element is "material" to the "meaning" of a photo, the discussion places us on a slippery slope. In a news photo, removing *any* objects large or small (or adding them, or rearranging them) without disclosure is a bad idea because it violates public expectations about the manner in which news photos reflect reality. When revealed, such manipulations erode credibility. The issue is not merely whether the alteration is *intended* to fool anyone, but also its potential for contributing to a loss of photocredibility.

The most ethically sound approach is to adhere to the viewfinder standard in news photos, to allow no exceptions for "mere distractions." (As described in later chapters, exceptions are allowed only when the image is so implausible as to fool no one anyway, or when the fiction is appropriately disclosed.) Note, however, that the viewfinder test is just a start. Adjusting depth-of-field or using wide-angle lenses or other tools or techniques could mislead viewers while still meeting the viewfinder test.

Beyond "Hard News"

Should we extend the viewfinder standard beyond news contexts, to other types of images in the nonfiction environment? The Explorations sections of Chapters 9, 10, and 11 examined a spectrum of implied authenticity among photos in different contexts: newspapers, magazine covers, etc. An individual's answers to questions concerning the *Men's Journal* "Spring Fever!" cover (Figure 10.2), *Time*'s "Deep Water" cover (Figure 10.3), *Newsweek*'s McCaughey septuplets cover (Figure 4.2), the *A Day in the Life* book cover (Figure 5.2), and other examples will help reveal where he or she draws the

> The concept of "best depiction" is too subjective for me (the concept is good; this is just a matter of degree, as I see it). We need to understand the limits imposed by the lens, films, etc. and work with these limits, but I do not think it proper in the context of news and documentary photojournalism to second-guess what is recorded. If a photo is viewed on a computer screen and the color of the sky is muddy (e.g., the <u>Challenger</u> explosion, where some papers removed the yellow printer to increase the contrast), the photographer has no right to say "I remember the color to be blue, so I will change what the film recorded," or "I want the color to be blue because it looks better and is easier to read."
>
> —John Long, former President, NPPA[3]

line between ethical photo illustration and deception. For example, some observers might make the following distinction:

- The context of the "Spring Fever!" cover (consumer magazine, travel feature) suggests that the photo's unnamed subjects are paid models who were hired, attired, "propped" and positioned by designers or photographers. The woman was made to appear topless by the removal of a bikini top tie across her back; whether the item was removed at the scene or later on a computer has little bearing on the image's implication of authenticity and is therefore ethically insignificant.
- The context and "Whitewater investigation" cover type in *Time* suggest that its photo was taken during Whitewater. Despite *Time*'s later explanation that the photo aptly portrayed the working relationship between President Clinton and George Stephanopoulos, the fact that the photo was taken at another time renders the cover misleading.

If responsible professionals disagree about altered images even in news contexts such as *Time* (or *Newsday, Newsweek, The New York Post, The Washington Post*, or any of the other news publications we have mentioned), then it is no wonder they disagree about altered images in other corners of the nonfiction environment where the rules have always been ambiguous.

NONFICTION PHOTOGRAPHY'S PROCESS TEST

Even people who have never heard of Photoshop and cannot tell an airbrush from a soldering gun have notions about "real" versus "manipulated" photography. In their minds, the former results from aiming the camera, pushing a button, developing the film, and printing the picture; the latter

An Application of the Darkroom Standard

From the official rules of the 2001–2002 William Randolph Hearst Foundation Journalism Awards Program:

> Images cannot be digitally altered beyond what is traditionally accepted in the darkroom. Computer-generated composites must be labeled as computer illustrations.

The following is permissible:

- Burning and dodging
- Improvement in contrast and/or lightening or darkening a photo to improve reproduction.
- Correcting technical defects in a photo by cloning pixels to cover dust spots or erase "line hits" [visual irregularities introduced by the process] in transmissions.
- Minor color changes to correct color shifts and improve reproduction quality. It is NOT permissible to alter the basic reality of a photograph.
- You cannot remove or insert objects from a photo.
- You cannot clone pixels to create a new image or add to an image.
- You cannot make radical color changes.

stems from some sort of trickery performed with fancy gear, darkroom chemicals, or razzle-dazzle software.

Close enough. For typical media consumers, the question is whether photographers or processors faked the photo, not how they did it. While decisions to select a subject, frame it, choose a lens, pick a photo for publication from a group of images, and so on all are interpretative acts, standard photographic and darkroom procedures nevertheless link photos to their subject matters in accepted ways, even if readers are fuzzy on the technical details.

If photography's credibility is to survive long into the digital age, mass-media images must pass "nonfiction photography's process test," the digital equivalent of traditional darkroom standards. That is, their processing must conform to the reader's Qualified Expectation of Reality; it must support the belief that standard procedures can be trusted to keep nonfiction photos at least as authentic as in the past. This requires updating the traditional darkroom standard discussed in Chapter 8.

Adapting the Darkroom Standard in News Contexts

When formulating guidelines for processing digital images, professionals point to film-based practices as good starting points. For example, the rules pertaining to the annual William Randolph Hearst Journalism Awards for student photography (see box) specify that "Images cannot be digitally altered beyond what is traditionally accepted in the darkroom." Likewise, the Associated Press maintains, "If we wouldn't do it in a darkroom, then we wouldn't do it on a computer. We might clean out some dust particles, that sort of thing, but otherwise we do not alter photos."[4]

Simply put, this darkroom standard adopts digital equivalents of the traditional techniques and concepts of photography's accepted grammar: cleaning and repairing negatives, dodging and burning, cropping that doesn't mislead, color correction, and particularly the imperfect yet helpful "altered content" versus "mere enhancement" distinction.

In a model application of these principles, the digital ethics policy of the Associated Press, says in part: "The content of a photograph will NEVER be changed or manipulated in any way. Only the established norms of standard photo printing methods such as burning, dodging, black-and-white toning and cropping are acceptable. Retouching is limited to removal of normal scratches and dust spots. Serious consideration must always be given in correcting color to ensure honest production of the original. Cases of abnormal color or tonality will be clearly stated in the caption."[5]

Taking the Darkroom Standard Beyond News Contexts

The discussion of extending the viewfinder standard beyond news contexts into other nonfiction areas is also applicable here. Whether we address what the photographer saw through the viewfinder or what the processor did in the lab or on the computer, the issue is the same: Given all aspects of context (the content of the photo, the reputation of the publication, cover type, and so on), what is the image's implication of authenticity? Does it meet that standard?

It was all white magic, I can't help thinking. The small adjustments to reality that occurred in Ansel Adams's darkroom, if crimes at all, were misdemeanors. That photographs should be "straightforward records of what the photographer witnessed and recorded on film in a single instant" [quoting photographer Gary Braasch's letter to the North American Nature Photography Association] still seems a worthy ideal, despite the fact that some of our greatest have stretched and jiggered it. Many fine principles are hallowed in the breach. That does not mean that they exert no influence, or that we should dispense with them entirely.

— Kenneth Brower, Atlantic Monthly[6]

SUMMARY

Several stages in the photographic process entail "manipulations" of some sort, or at least a degree of subjectivity, but whether we call it manipulation, alteration, or enhancement, the key issue is whether it misleads viewers. Regardless of whether an alteration occurs pre- or post-exposure, and regardless of whether the technique is chemical, mechanical, or digital, the issue is the same: Given the context, what is the image's implication of authenticity? Does it meet that standard?

Future challenges will be especially acute because many of tomorrow's decision makers will have no more familiarity with film or darkroom conventions than they have with manual typewriters. But with a rudimentary grasp of journalistic principles, they can continue to apply new image processing techniques in ethical ways.

EXPLORATIONS

1. The "but it's just a tiny detail" argument was heard in regard to the removal of the Diet Coke can from the *St. Louis Post-Dispatch* photo (Figure 10.1). The newspaper's defenders might argue that, after all, the photo and its accompanying text had nothing to do with soft drinks. The can was off to the side. Deleting it from within the frame was a minor alteration, an aesthetic improvement. It actually made the photo *more* credible by eliminating a distraction that might draw undue attention to itself or even appear to be a direct or indirect product endorsement. The alteration kept the focus on the subject of the story, where it belonged. It did not change the photo's meaning.

    But critics argued that *any* removal of a material object changes a photo's perceived relationship to reality, that is, its meaning. The item in question need not be an essential object, and the alteration does not have to fool readers intentionally. While the Coke can may be "merely" a detail, the journalist's obligation is to reflect reality, not to reconstruct it to conform to the whims of some art director. The alteration violated the expectations of readers, who believe that a journalistic photo captures what the photographer saw, not what he or she might have seen under different circumstances. Regardless of whether the *intent* is to mislead, taking objects out of a journalistic photo—or inserting them or rearranging them—is (a) unethical, because it misleads the public, and (b) unwise, because it undermines faith in journalism.

    Does either view reflect your opinion? With respect to the *St. Louis Post-Dispatch* photo, how would you answer Bill Moyers's question: "Is this journalism?"

2. Regarding the previous question, suppose the photographer had removed the soda can from the scene prior to taking the photo. How would such an action differ, if at all, from optically removing the can from the frame later?

3. The Associated Press is a global news gathering and news dissemination organization. Its policy states: "The content of a photograph will NEVER be changed. . . . Only the established norms of standard photo printing methods. . . are acceptable." Is that standard comprehensive enough to serve as a guideline for any newspaper's photographers and editors? Would it make sense to apply it to photos appearing in news magazine feature stories? On news magazine covers? In general interest consumer magazine features? On general interest consumer magazine covers? In online magazines or newspapers? In each case, why or why not?

4. The 2001–2002 Hearst Journalism Awards rules (see box on page 144) specify that submitted photos "cannot be altered digitally or in any other way that changes the content." Specify examples of processing or alterations that would, and would not, constitute changes in content. Would the Hearst guideline serve as a useful starting point for all visual journalists?

ENDNOTES

1. Paul Lester, *Readings in Mass Communication*, 1995, http://commfaculty.fullerton.edu/lester/writings/photoethics.html.
2. From an e-mail correspondence with the author, fall 1998.
3. From an e-mail correspondence with the author, fall 1998.
4. Interview with Jack Smith of Portland, Oregon's, AP bureau, July 7, 1994.
5. *News Photographer* (September 1997): 7.
6. Kenneth Brower, "Photography in the Age of Falsification," *Atlantic Monthly* (May 1998): 96.

Chapter 14

Photofiction Tests 3 and 4

The Technical Credibility and
Obvious Implausibility Tests

If the cover is an illustration, it had better look like one.
—Joseph R. Traver, *President,* NPPA[1]

THE TECHNICAL CREDIBILITY TEST

In the days before digital imaging, sloppy cutouts of celebrities sometimes graced the covers of supermarket tabloids. A titillating juxtaposition or even a scandalous liaison could be "exposed" with the publishing equivalent of scissors and library paste. Sometimes looking as if five-year-olds had thrown them together, such images were not credible and, we may hope, seldom misled readers. In a way, their very shortcomings were a contrast to, and might have helped protect, the credibility of legitimate photography.

Back in that predigital era, creating seemingly coherent composites required skill, long hours, and expensive equipment. But now, with moderate skill and effort, a nearly seamless "photograph" can be contrived on the desktop at home. Even head transplants are readily accomplished. When *Texas Monthly* published a composite photo of gubernatorial candidates Clayton Williams and Ann Richards apparently dancing together (Figure 14.1), or when it published a composite photo of Richards' head on a leather-clad body sitting on a motorcycle (Chapter 4), the results were so well crafted that only skilled eyes could detect the manipulations.

The technical credibility test may rarely come into play, because current software permits concocting realistic photofiction with modest skill, expense and effort. Nonetheless, the key question is: Does shoddy execution alert viewers to the manipulation?

FIGURE 14.1.   An image may be somewhat surprising yet not "obviously implausible" as the term is used in this chapter. For many viewers, this "head transplant" composite looked like a real photo that seemed to reveal that bitter political rivals Clayton Williams and Ann Richards had once been friends.

OBVIOUS IMPLAUSIBILITY: THE "PREGNANT BRUCE WILLIS" TEST

As pointed out in Chapter 12, the reader's Qualified Expectation of Reality may allow for photofiction in nonfiction environments so long as it is (1) appropriately disclosed, or (2) obviously implausible and therefore in no need of disclosure. When the fiction is obvious, the QER is not violated. It is suspended altogether: There *is* no expectation of reality in an obviously unreal "photo." Reasonably well-informed readers recognize visual jokes or obvious photo-illustrations when they see them in satirical, fictional or even journalistic settings:

- They know that the two-faced image on the cover of *Newsweek*'s November 20, 2000, issue was a composite of presidential candidates George W. Bush and Al Gore.
- They know that the tiny handgun in the eye of a teenager on *Time*'s "How to Spot a Troubled Teen" cover (May 31, 1999) must have been put there by an artist.
- They know that some sort of digital or darkroom magic was applied to the cover of October 1998's *Psychology Today*, in which part of the model's face appears on the back of her hand (Figure 14.2).
- They know that software tycoon Bill Gates and antitrust lawyer Joel Klein are not old-fashioned prizefighters as depicted in *Time*'s June 1, 1998, boxing-poster layout (Figure 14.3).

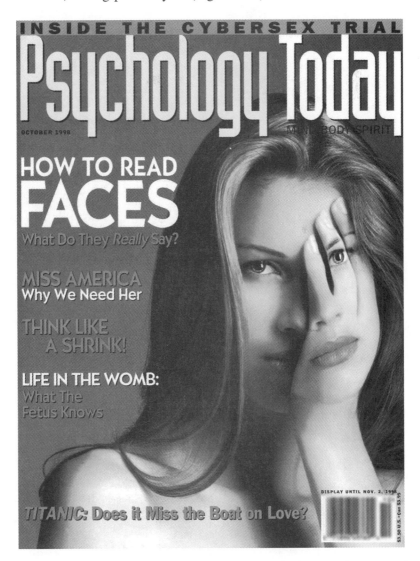

FIGURE 14.2. Obvious photofiction: Readers need not be told that this seemingly "photorealistic" creation is in fact fictional. Copyright © 1994 Gerald Bybee.

- They know that Queen Elizabeth does not have a nose ring (*Allure*, February 1995, page 62).
- They know that *Life*'s October 1992 cover image is a composite or some other manipulation (Figure 14.4). To illustrate its "Can We Stop Aging?" feature, the magazine blended two photos of the same woman taken in 1944 and 1992.
- They know that O.J. Simpson is not the blonde, blue-eyed Caucasian pictured on *Wired*'s September 1995 cover.
- They know that the black and white women have had their heads switched in the bizarre June/July 1997 *Detour* magazine fashion

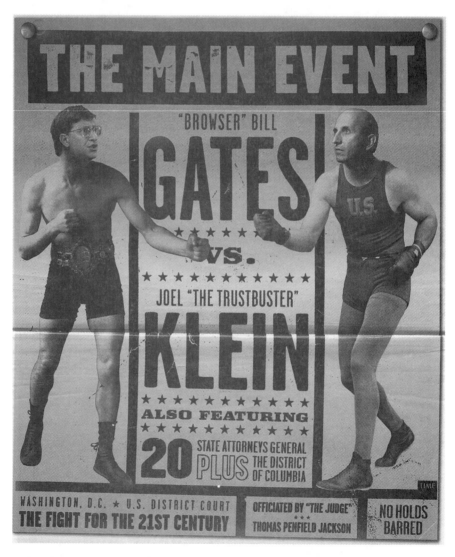

FIGURE 14.3.   For more than a century, cartoonists have pictured political or legal opponents as boxers. With computers, such illustrations can be rendered photoreal-istically, as in this image of software giant Bill Gates and antitrust lawyer Joel Klein.

FIGURE 14.4. This compelling blend of photos taken in 1944 and 1992 would be recognized by typical readers as some sort of composite, so it does not violate ethical journalism's long-held commitment to truthfulness.

spread (if the mismatched skin colors did not reveal the transplant, the crude, simulated stitches around the models' necks certainly would).

- If they are familiar with Bob Jackson's famous photo of Jack Ruby shooting a wincing Lee Harvey Oswald, they will surely identify as parody George Mahlberg's altered version, in which Ruby wields an electric guitar rather than a handgun, and Oswald is "screamin' the blues" into a microphone.[2]
- Perhaps the ultimate example is that readers know that actor Bruce Willis can't be pregnant (*Spy* cover, September 1991), and they need not be told that the image was falsified (Figure 14.5).

The obvious implausibility test involves this key question: Is the fictional content of the photo (or photolike image) so obvious that it readily tips off viewers as to the manipulation? If so, its publication may be perfectly responsible, even without prominent disclosure. Of course, this is not to say that such photofiction is therefore tasteful, smart, or appropriate for every

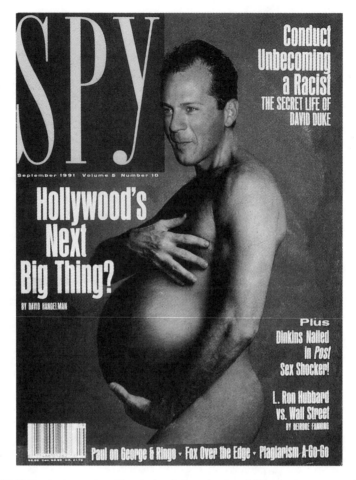

FIGURE 14.5.   Perhaps the ultimate in obvious implausibility, Spy's pregnant Bruce Willis cover was a parody of a Vanity Fair cover featuring Willis's pregnant wife, Demi Moore.

publication's mission or identity, but simply that it may breach no ethical standard.

Impossible Juxtapositions

Some altered images reveal their fictions by portraying familiar people or scenes in stunningly unfamiliar ways, such as the February 1994 cover of *Scientific American* picturing Marilyn Monroe on the arm of Abraham Lincoln (Figure 14.6), or the television commercial in which the late John Wayne joins contemporary actors in a tavern. As mentioned in Chapter 5, such concoctions—in advertising, journalism, or satire—are modern equivalents of the Mona Lisa with a graffiti mustache: We know enough about the real thing to recognize the manipulation. These altered images thus pass the

FIGURE 14.6.   A common type of photo manipulation pictures unlikely or (as in this case) impossible pairings of familiar people or scenes.

test of obvious implausibility; their publication, even without prominent disclosure, breaches no ethical standard.

Failing the Test

The clues of implausibility evident in the Monroe/Lincoln composite or the pregnant Bruce Willis "photo" were lacking, however, in several now notorious cases of photofiction. One example is *Time*'s blurred and darkened O.J. Simpson cover (Chapter 4), which confused some viewers and offended many critics. Richard Smith, *Newsweek*'s editor in chief, said that *Time* "didn't change it *enough* to make it clear it was an illustration" (emphasis added).[3]

If it seems ironic that a heavily manipulated photo might be more ethical than a lightly manipulated one, it is because the former may be so implausible or look so manipulated that it has little potential for misleading

FIGURE 14.7.   The image on the opposite page appeared in the Sunday <u>New York Times Magazine</u>. Photographer/artist Troy House reports, "The original studio shot [this page] didn't look that real to begin with, but the <u>Times</u> wanted to make sure no one would mistake it for a real photo, so we re-did it. We brought in some cartoon elements, dramatic angles, gave it that super-hero look. It caused quite a stir, and everyone liked it."

readers. Janet Froelich, art director for the Sunday *New York Times Magazine*, cited an altered image that was repeatedly sent back to digital artists to make it look *less* plausible, until the editor was satisfied that its fictional content was so obvious that no one would be misled (Figure 14.7).[4]

WHEN IS FICTION OBVIOUS?

How obvious must the fiction be to justify running a photofictional image without unambiguous disclosure? Must it be obvious to at least a substantial minority of viewers? A large majority? Virtually all of them?

There is no single answer. Such judgment calls depend upon the editor's willingness to mislead or confuse at least a few readers for the sake of impressing others with an arresting illustration. These decisions may also

depend on the mission of the publication and the perceived sophistication of its audience.

THE OREGON STUDY

Of course, audience awareness is difficult to ascertain. In one attempt, 430 University of Oregon students were surveyed as to their reactions to various "photos," some hypothetical, some actual, and some actual but manipulated. In the survey's instructions, the term "composite photo" was defined, and respondents were told the following: "The images shown . . . may or may not be composites."[5]

One publication, the satirical *Spy*, was selected because the survey designer believed respondents would be more likely to assume that its cover images were manipulated. The students viewed the magazine's Daryl Hannah cover (Figure 14.8), a manipulated composite that was explained as follows (quoted descriptions of publications are from *Bacon's Magazine Directory*):

First Lady Jackie Kennedy was wearing a pink suit like the one shown here at the time her husband, President John F. Kennedy, was assassinated in Dallas in

FIGURE 14.8.   Actress Daryl Hannah never posed for this computer-composited image, but some readers were fooled and wrote in to complain about her participation in the controversial design.

1963. Actress Daryl Hannah, pictured here, has been romantically linked to the late President's son, John F. Kennedy Jr. The caption to this cover photo reads "Daryl Hannah as Mrs. John F. Kennedy Jr.?" *Spy* is an irreverent, satirical magazine covering "personalities, institutions, and culture in urban America."

The respondents, most of whom were among the magazine's target market, were asked: "How likely is it that this picture is a composite or 'trick' photo?"

They were asked the same question regarding *Esquire*'s January 1994 cover, which pictured a woman nude from the waist up, her breasts cupped by hands belonging to an otherwise concealed person behind her (Figure 14.9). One of the hands was wearing a sequined glove, a trademark of singer Michael Jackson, who was the subject of a scandal at the time and who was mentioned on the magazine's cover. The photo was explained as follows:

FIGURE 14.9.   Several clues suggested to some readers that this parody of a Rolling Stone cover was a Spy-type composite, but it is a real photo.

This cover photo of so-called "Hollywood Madam" Heidi Fleiss appeared on *Esquire*'s annual Dubious Achievement Awards issue. It followed by several months a similar image of singer Janet Jackson on the cover of *Rolling Stone*. *Esquire* addresses "the changing role of the American male in today's society" and covers current events, trends, fashion, profiles and fiction.

We may not find it surprising that 58% of the respondents thought *Spy*'s Daryl Hannah image was "very likely" or "somewhat likely" to be a composite, given its outrageousness and implausibility, not to mention *Spy*'s reputation for satire. Still, more than one-third thought it was somewhat or very *unlikely* to be a composite—that is, many respondents were wrong. Regarding the Heidi Fleiss cover, *most* of the respondents were wrong: Sixty percent thought it was "very likely" or "somewhat likely" to be a composite, which it was not.[6]

Regarding a hypothetical manipulation of a photo of the 1969 moon landing in which the American flag was replaced with the Japanese flag: "If I were doing a column — 'What if the Japanese Had Been the First to Land on the Moon?'— I could illustrate it with that image. . . . The reader would know that this was indeed an illustration. . . . But you have to be smart in the way that you use it, and you have to send clear signals to the readers [about] exactly what they're looking at."

—Janet Froelich, The New York Times Magazine[7]

SUMMARY

The technical credibility and obvious implausibility tests are similar: In the former, the image's shoddy execution may alert readers to its fictional aspects, while in the latter its palpably unrealistic content may do the same. The ethical issue in either case is whether the viewer is likely to recognize the image as fictional. If the image falls short of being obviously implausible, it is potentially misleading, and a lack of disclosure risks diminished credibility.

There may be no expectation of reality in an obviously unreal photo, but at what point does the fiction become apparent enough to put readers on alert? This is a matter of editorial taste and judgment.

The Oregon research sample is small and unrepresentative, but like readers' erroneous assumptions that some real photos are manipulated,[8] and like the observation that manipulated images undermine the credibility of real photos,[9] the Oregon study raises important questions: If readers suspect that real photos are manipulated, or that manipulated photos are real, what are the implications for the survival of nonfiction mass-media photography? What can visual journalists do about it?

EXPLORATIONS

1. When *Spy* in February 1993 published a photorealistic cover image of Hillary Clinton's head on the body of a whip-brandishing model dressed in a leather bikini and fishnet stockings, was it safe to assume that the majority of regular *Spy* readers were in on the joke? What about passersby who saw the magazine on newsstands or store shelves? Would your assumption differ in regard to them?

   Consider *Spy*'s Hillary Clinton, Bruce Willis (Figure 14.5) and Daryl Hannah (Figure 14.8) covers: Of casual viewers seeing them on a magazine rack, estimate the percentage who would immediately recognize the fiction in each case. If your estimates vary from example to example, explain why: What kinds of clues make photofiction recognizable?

Would such estimates be reasonable factors in deciding whether to publish examples of photofiction? Would diminishing estimates suggest at some point that use of the image is probably unethical? At what point? Finally, how might the effect of these photos have differed had they appeared in contexts other than *Spy*?

2. Before reading the discussion of the Oregon survey, did you assume the Heidi Fleiss image was real or a fake? Was your answer influenced either by knowing it was a parody of the *Rolling Stone* Janet Jackson cover, or by its appearance on *Esquire*'s Dubious Achievement Awards issue? Can you think of other examples of how references to previous images or other aspects of photographic context might suggest obvious or at least possible photofiction?

3. Collect examples of obvious or suspected photofiction appearing in any purportedly nonfiction print medium—consumer magazines, newspapers, etc. What clues tip off viewers as to the fictional content of the images? How obvious is the fiction? How are the images labeled, if at all?

ENDNOTES

1. Letters, *Time* (July 18, 1994): 5.
2. *Wired* (August 1997): 104.
3. Howard Kurtz, "*Time*'s 'Sinister' Simpson; Cover Photo Was Computer-Enhanced," *The Washington Post* (June 22, 1994): Style, D1.
4. From an interview with the author; the image appeared in the magazine's January 7, 1996, issue, 45.
5. Tom Wheeler, "Public Perceptions of Photographic Credibility in the Age of Digital Manipulation," a paper presented to the annual convention of the Association for Education in Journalism and Mass Communication (AEJMC), Washington, D.C., August 1995.
6. The *Spy* digital composite was identified inside the magazine as a "paintbox photo composition." The Fleiss photo was discussed in the "Backstage with Esquire" column, so anyone misled by the cover would have been set straight by reading that column.
7. "Forum Focus: Photo-journalism or Photo-fiction," a video produced by the Freedom Forum, 1101 Wilson Blvd., Arlington, Virginia 22209; 1995.
8. For example, the Mary Ellen Mark photo in *Condé Nast Traveler*, cited in Chapter 4.
9. In Chapter 4, *Texas Monthly* art director D.J. Stout reported that ". . . altered photographs were really hurting the integrity of the magazine's cover . . . when we had a great photograph, nobody believed it."

Chapter 15

The Wording of a Disclosure

We've got to hammer away at the idea that certain publications have uses of photographs as representations of reality. It's not an easy road. Credibility will likely continue to erode, and our job will get harder. I'm at a loss to know what to suggest, except to be a good example, and to remind people in the "realistic photography" business that it's in their interests to preserve this niche. We have an obligation not only to the readers of today but also in the long term. If in a hundred years someone picks up a National Geographic, *or a book by Art Wolfe, or even an advertisement that purports to reflect reality, we need to find a way to inform those readers of the future that this is a document, a record of what the world was like at that moment.*

—Bill Allen, *National Geographic*[1]

IN THE INTEREST OF FULL DISCLOSURE . . .

It was noted in Chapter 11 in a comparison of photos to text that some altered quotes might be deemed ethical if accompanied by an explanation, such as, "The following interview was conducted over a two-day period and has been condensed for brevity and edited for continuity." Similarly, it has often been suggested that some sort of label or disclaimer would render manipulated photography ethically acceptable in journalism.

Wildlife photographer Art Wolfe's book *Migrations* included a number of digitally altered photos that were criticized by other photographers. Wolfe reported, "Since then we've published another book, *In the Presence of Wolves*, with five digital illustrations that were labeled as such, and no one objected. So we figured out that people were upset less because we used the technology than because we did not always say we had."[2] This revelation hardly seems surprising: With adequate disclosure readers are informed; without it they are duped.

In attempts to avoid misleading readers about photofiction or simply to acknowledge contributors, publications have used different labels, located in different places. Even back in the 1920s, *The Evening Graphic* called its composite photos "composographs," identified them as products of the paper's art department, and sometimes admitted in very fine print that the images were faked.[3]

Time's March 25, 1996, "Can Machines Think?" cover was identified on the contents page as a "digital photomontage" (Figure 15.1). *Time*'s January 29, 2001, issue addressed the energy crisis in California; its cover pictured

FIGURE 15.1. Visual communicators use a variety of terms to label their computerized images. This one was identified on the contents page as a "digital photomontage."

a multi-plug power strip in the shape of the state and was also labeled "digital photomontage."

The September 28, 1997, *New York Times Magazine* contained a four-panel photo-based illustration of how Daniel Lee saw his own facial features evolving along a continuum from the distant past into the future; aside from technical information that might interest illustrators, examples like this "evolutionary self-portrait" need no disclosure.

Accompanying the January/February 1999 *Maxim* magazine article "Muscle up by March" was a single-frame photo with multiple images showing a pudgy fellow morphing into a hunky stud, requisite rock-hard abs and all; the simple credit line, "Imaging, Gene Bresler," seemed adequate.

Given its reputation for outrageous satire, it is ironic that *Spy* magazine is more straightforward than some news publications in identifying manipulated photography. Its photofictional covers have been identified on interior pages with such terms as "computer imaging" (December 1994), "paintbox photo composition" (February 1993), and "cover by Digital Facelifts, Inc." (June 1995).

THE ELEMENTS OF DISCLOSURE

Unless they meet the test of obvious implausibility, examples of photofiction in journalistic environments require some sort of disclosure. (In his 1999 reader awareness study, Edgar Huang reported, "Almost 100% of the respondents expect the media to let them know if a digitally altered image was used. . . . Promoting such awareness could better legitimize potential alterations."[4]) A brief but reasonably specific qualifier such as "digitally altered" would often be adequate, and hardly a burden on publications already crediting photographers and sometimes people responsible for hair, makeup, fashions and so on.

Another logical element would be the name of the person or company who effected the manipulation: "Photo by Bob Schuter; digital alteration by Foto Fantasy, Inc." As with photographers, the contributions of retouchers and digital artists should not go uncredited.

A final element could cite the source material, if applicable: "from a photo by Ansel Adams." (Of course, failure to credit copyrighted source images is not only unethical but illegal.) Regarding the O.J. Simpson cover (Chapter 4), Joseph P. Kahn reported: "If *Time* erred at all, says [the art director], it was in failing to credit the L.A.P.D. mug shot on which [the] illustration was based, leaving readers to guess at the source of the original image."[5] Matt Mahurin, creator of the Simpson "photo-illustration," agreed.[6]

One exemplary attribution accompanied *Newsweek*'s December 22, 1997, cover image of Princess Diana, credited as a "photomosaic . . . from a photograph by Alpha/Globe Photos." In another, *Mother Jones'* December 1994 cover, an illustration of President Clinton as a battered boxer, bore the credit line: "Cover illustration by Daniel Lee, based on photo by Gamma Liaison."

"PHOTO-ILLUSTRATIONS"

Time's 1994 O.J. Simpson cover is particularly relevant here for two reasons: It is the best known example of altered photography in recent years, and it was identified on an interior page as a "photo-illustration." Let's

> A visual lie is a visual lie, no matter how you caption it. There is not an editor alive who would write in italics at the end of a story about a drug addicted child in Washington D.C. that "the kid himself did not exist but since we needed to personalize the very real problem, we created a composite kid, so the story is valid because we told you it was fake." This is what we are doing when we try to caption away visual lies with disclaimers like "photo illustration."
>
> —John Long, former President, NPPA, referring to "Jimmy's World," a fabricated story about an 8-year-old heroin addict that appeared in 1980 in The Washington Post.[7]

examine this common term. The hyphen suggests the image is part photo, part illustration—perhaps a photo altered with pencils, paints, or software. But aren't actual, unaltered photos often used for "illustrative" purposes? When is even a news photo *not* an "illustration" of some kind? Is it really safe to assume that readers agree that "illustrations" are always drawings, paintings, computer creations, or the like?

Another question is whether readers notice or go to the trouble to seek out fine-print disclaimers. Even more basic, do they know what "photo-illustration" means when they come across it? Of course, they do not. How could they? Within the profession we ourselves do not know what it means, or, more precisely, we do not agree on a single meaning. How then could the public agree on one? Commenting on the Simpson cover, *The Washington Post* judged the term unfamiliar enough to require putting it in quotes: "[The] photo was electronically manipulated to create what *Time*, in small type on the contents page, calls a 'photo illustration.' "[8] In the July 4, 1994, "To Our Readers" column, *Time*'s managing editor deemed it necessary to explain the term: "using photography as the basis for work in another medium, in this case a computerized image."

The problem is not that *Time*'s definition is deficient but rather that it is only one of several. *The Register-Guard* newspaper in Eugene, Oregon, ran a cooking story accompanied by a photo of a chef, his arms folded across his chest, a carving knife in one hand.[9] No elements within the frame were added, removed, substantially altered, or rearranged. It was no secret that the photo was posed (the chef looked straight into the lens), and the meaning of the photo was not changed during processing. In other words, this portrait was a "real" photo, not photofiction; it meant what it said. And yet it was identified in large type as a photo-illustration only because, as the photographer later explained, "It wasn't capturing or documenting a news event; we posed it for a feature."[10] The photographer and his paper are to be commended. If every publication acted so diligently to protect the legitimacy of nonfiction photography, perhaps its credibility would not be endangered.

Labels

A five-member committee appointed by New York University's Program on Copyright and the New Technologies recommended in early 1996 that different types of images be marked with appropriate labels:

- unaltered photos ("photo-reportage")
- posed photos ("photo-portraits")
- pictures in which elements were arranged ("photo-illustrations")
- pictures taken under imposed restrictions ("photo opportunities")
- cosmetic alterations ("retouched")
- pictures in which objects are added or subtracted ("composite")
- non-photo-based computer illustrations ("computer-generated image").[11]

For substantially manipulated photos, Tony Stone Images, a stock photo company, uses labels such as Digital Composite (when components have been added, deleted, or moved), Digital Enhancement, and Color Enhancement.[12]

Professor Fred Ritchin pointed out that "photo-illustration" has also been applied to an image in which models play the roles of people covered in an article.[13] In yet another application, the term described a *USA Today* set-up photo in which a prop was used; the "prop" was a harmless white powder apparently being snorted by a young student at her locker. The headline read: "Teens and Drugs: In a classroom of 25, three kids are users."[14]

For some publications, then, "photo-illustration" may identify photos that are posed or "propped" but unmanipulated in the lab. For others, it can identify photos manipulated so heavily they look like paintings. While not entirely useless, the term falls short as a commonly acknowledged identifier of photofiction.

HOW MUCH SPECIFICITY?

For most editors, space on a page is precious, so attributions or labels are typically brief. Still, some specificity is necessary. "Computer-enhanced photo" might mislead readers to believe that a fictional image is real but merely enhanced, more or less in the way photos have been responsibly "enhanced" in darkrooms for decades.

"Digital photo-illustration" is marginally better, although some might misinterpret it to indicate an unmanipulated photo taken with a digital camera.

Even a seemingly comprehensive label such as "Composite photo-illustration" may be insufficient. J.D. Lasica reported that when that term was applied to an image in the *Asbury Park Press*, its design director confessed, "some people were left scratching their heads."[15]

PLAIN TALK AND LARGER TRUTHS

The words "retouched," "altered," "manipulated," and their variants are widely understood and can serve as adequate disclosures, often in conjunction with "montage," "mosaic," "composite," or the marginally useful "photo-illustration." If during processing the photographer fictionalizes his or her own photo, a single term crediting both contributions would be in order. "Computer-retouched photo-illustration," "digitally altered photo montage," or "computer-manipulated composite photo" would all seem sufficiently specific to inform readers yet brief enough to satisfy editors.

Readers and writers of literature claim that fiction can convey a "larger truth." No argument here, but don't readers want to know whether they are reading fiction or nonfiction? Are viewers of photos any different? In journalistic text, when fiction masquerades as nonfiction the results can range from embarrassment to disgrace, even shattered careers or lawsuits. How can we avoid similar disasters with respect to journalistic images?

If the words "manipulated" or "fiction" are applicable, let's embrace them. Let's inform our readers, and they can make up their own minds as to an image's larger truth. After all, there's nothing unethical about fiction—literary or visual—so long as it is not passed off as nonfiction. Like novelists, responsible creators of photofiction have nothing to hide. It makes no more sense for them to disguise their work as nonfiction than for Dostoevsky or Vonnegut to have done the same. In many cases, then, a disclaimer such as "computerized photo-manipulation" would serve well, or even better, "computerized photofiction."

ICONS

In 1994, New York University's Interactive Telecommunications Program proposed a system of icons to identify both altered and unaltered photos. The American Society of Media Photographers (formerly the American Society of Magazine Photographers) supported the plan, as did the British union of journalists, Italy's *Airone* magazine, and individual photographers

> It is inappropriate to use a photo-illustration with a news story. Even if you mark it clearly, the reader tends to be misled. It's that simple.
>
> — Nancy Lee, <u>The New York Times</u>[16]

and agencies. As explained by the ASMP, the icons are a boxed zero, indicating that the photo was made "with the lens," and a boxed zero with a slash through it, indicating a manipulation.[17]

As Ritchin explained,

> We felt that [the fundamental difference] between a photograph and a manipulated photograph is the lens, and that the lens has been supplanted by digital or even conventional technologies . . . [The intention is] not to say that the photograph is better or worse than the manipulation, but to point out that it represents a different strategy.[18]

(Because it supported the Ritchin/NYU proposal, the ASMP dropped its own recommendation that the mathematical symbol for "unequal," an equal sign crossed with a slash, be adopted to identify altered photography.[19])

In the July/August 1995 *American Photo* poll (Chapter 4), readers were asked if they thought using the "not a lens" icon on manipulated photos is "a good idea." The tallies were: yes, 81; no, 9; not sure, 7; no comment, 6.

Based in the United Kingdom, the National Union of Journalists is the largest organization of its kind, with some 25,000 members. In October 1996 it launched a campaign to make sure every digitally manipulated photo appearing in a newspaper or magazine bears an identifying "not a camera" mark; it also proposed a "genuine photo" icon for unmanipulated photos.

SUMMARY

The profession has failed to settle upon consistent guidelines for disclosing photofiction. The term "photo-illustration" is often used, despite its shortcomings. The icon proposal has yet to catch on.

Effective disclosures include clear, unambiguous language; perhaps the name of the person or company who rendered the alteration; and, if applicable, credit for source material. While editors may differ as to the necessity of specifying exactly how the manipulation was accomplished, the key requirement is that the wording prevents the image from misleading viewers. Another aspect, the disclosure's prominence, is addressed in the next chapter.

EXPLORATIONS

1. Discuss in terms of Aristotle's Golden Mean (Chapter 6) a manipulated photo whose fiction is disclosed to readers.

2. Bring to class examples of manipulated photography identified with some sort of label ("photo-illustration," "digitally altered," etc.). How many different wordings can you find? In each case, how do the type of publication and the type of image seem to relate to the wording of the disclosure?

3. In the January 1997 PBS program *Media Matters*, former *Life* managing editor Daniel Okrent speculated that icons might cause more problems than they solve: "Once you put a word on that, like a label, then you have to be prepared for the reader to believe that you have invented the whole thing." In other words, readers could not tell which parts of the image were fictional and which were real, negating the point of the entire photo. Do you agree?

4. Some members of the National Press Photographers Association opposed the icon concept because they felt it might legitimize a practice that is inherently dishonest. In other words, if manipulating a photo is wrong, don't do it—period. What do you think?

Chapter 6 explained, "Ethical systems also typically entail enumerating a set of valued actions or behaviors and then providing guidelines for determining when, if ever, exceptions are tolerated." Which of the principles addressed in that discussion would support the notion that if it's wrong, don't do it—no exceptions?

ENDNOTES

1. From an e-mail correspondence with the author, fall 1998.
2. Kenneth Brower, "Photography in the Age of Falsification," *Atlantic Monthly* (May 1998): 107.
3. The caption to the outrageous Rhinelander trial Composograph (Chapter 2) was admirably forthcoming, explaining that the image was "carefully prepared from a description given by one of the witnesses." Bob Stepno, "Staged, Faked and Mostly Naked: Photographic Innovation at the Evening Graphic (1924–1932)," graduate student paper (School of Journalism and Mass Communication, University of North Carolina at Chapel Hill), presented at the annual convention of the Association for Education in Journalism and Mass Communication (AEJMC), Visual Communication Division, Chicago, 1997, 7.
4. Edgar Shaohua Huang, "Readers' Perception of Digital Alteration and Truth-Value in Documentary Photographs," submitted in partial fulfillment for a Ph.D. degree, School of Journalism, Indiana University (October 1999): 182–83.
5. See Joseph P. Kahn, "When 1 Picture Tells 2 Stories," *The Boston Globe* (June 22, 1994): Living, p. 21.
6. Janet Abrams, "Little Photoshop of Horrors: The Ethics of Manipulating Journalistic Imagery," *Print* (November/December 1995): 26.
7. From an e-mail correspondence with the author, fall 1998.
8. Howard Kurtz, "*Time*'s 'Sinister' Simpson; Cover Photo Was Computer-Enhanced," *The Washington Post* (June 22, 1994): Style, D1.
9. *The Register-Guard*, Eugene, Oregon (April 19, 1995): D-1.
10. From an interview with the author, April 21, 1995.
11. "Standards for Photography's Cutting Edge," *Washington Journalism Review* (November 1992): 12.
12. News Beat, "Digital Manipulation Meets Truth in Labeling," *Publish* (February 1996).
13. Fred Ritchin, "It's Not News Anymore When a Photo Is Art," *New York Newsday* (June 30, 1994).
14. G. Bruce Knecht, "At USA Today, a Staged Photo Isn't Good News," *The Wall Street Journal* (August 22, 1996): B1. The powder was actually not visible in the image. In any case, editor David Mazzarella admitted the posed photo was a mistake. It appeared in *USA Today*'s cover story on August 21, 1996.
15. J.D. Lasica, "Photographs That Lie: The Ethical Dilemma of Digital Retouching," *Washington Journalism Review* (June 1989): 24.
16. Nancy Lee is the picture editor at *The New York Times*. Knecht, B7.
17. *ASMP Bulletin*, June 1994, 17.
18. Abrams, 25.
19. Author's interview with Peter Skinner, editor, *ASMP Bulletin*, July 6, 1994. See also *ASMP Bulletin*, June 1994, 17.

Chapter 16

The Prominence of a Disclosure

Test 5: The "Essence of the Image"

Newspapers are read on the run, and people don't inspect credit lines.
—Sig Gissler, Columbia University[1]

SOMETIMES FINE PRINT IS INSUFFICIENT

Once we agree upon the wording of a disclosure, what sort of format or placement is appropriate? Is fine print adequate? If the disclosure merely acknowledges a contributor's effort and refers either to obvious photofiction or to an alteration so slight as to mislead no one, there's no reason "computer alteration by Digital Magic, Inc." should be any more prominent than a photographer's credit. For example, regarding the digital removal of actor Don Johnson's handgun and holster from a 1985 *Rolling Stone* cover,[2] a sentence fragment in the photo credit line on the contents page would have done the job (Figure 16.1).

But sometimes fine print is insufficient, as when a realistic-looking image falls outside readers' expectations and is some sort of composite, visual speculation, or other substantially altered contrivance. If the disclosure is necessary to avoid misleading readers, then it requires some degree of prominence to be effective.

TONYA AND NANCY

After skater Tonya Harding was implicated in an assault on rival Nancy Kerrigan, many people speculated about what might occur when the two athletes met at the Olympics in Norway. *New York Newsday* reported the juicy story before its competitors could do so; indeed, it reported the story before it happened. On February 16, 1994, the day before the skaters' much anticipated joint practice at the rink in Lillehammer, *Newsday* filled its cover page with a photolike image, under the headline "Fire on Ice." It

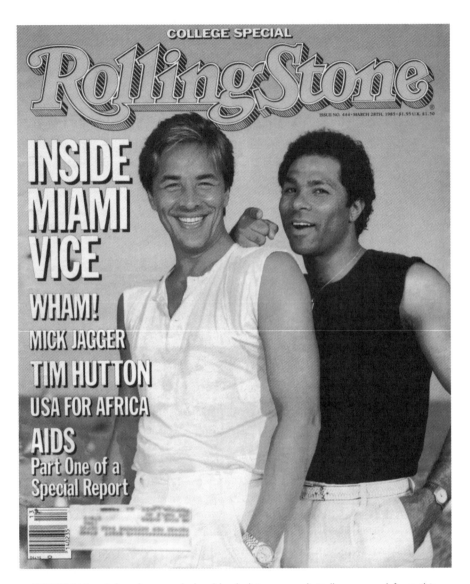

FIGURE 16.1.   A handgun and shoulder holster were digitally removed from this photo of Don Johnson and his Miami Vice co-star—a substantial alteration, but one that would fail the "essence of the image" test.

appeared to show the women skating side by side—a story millions seemed to be clamoring for, a story no other publication could provide. In fact, the image was a composite. The relatively fine-print caption on the same page revealed that Harding and Kerrigan "appear to skate together in this *New York Newsday* composite." The disclosure was certainly better than nothing. Was it sufficient?

New York Newsday editor Donald Forst said, "There is nothing wrong with illustration—and using the magic of electronics to do so—so long as it is understood as such." But was it understood as such? Even *Newsday* editor

> I don't think newspapers or magazines do a good job of help-
> ing readers understand various types of images. Nor do they
> help readers understand why and how changes are made to
> original images. In fact, given disagreement within news orga-
> nizations, it's not surprising that we don't communicate clearly
> to readers. First, organizations need to have greater clarity of
> what they stand for, their principles and values. Then they need
> clear, functional guidelines and protocols for daily decision
> making. Beyond that, I believe editors should systematically
> and regularly offer readers a more detailed explanation on
> such matters as photo-illustrations, credits, disclaimers, etc.
> (though I hate the word "disclaimer" since it means "we don't
> claim responsibility," which is unacceptable).
>   — Bob Steele, The Poynter Institute[3]

Anthony Marro said, "I have to admit, when I picked up the paper on my
front porch, I said, 'Uh-oh, it looked very real.' "[4]

IMPLICATIONS OF AUTHENTICITY AND
THE ESSENCE OF THE IMAGE

Throughout various chapters, this book has acknowledged that mass-media
images' implications of authenticity vary substantially according to context.
Generally, we cannot ascertain the ethics of an alteration without knowing
how the photo is to be used.

A useful corollary to this discussion is an examination of the relative
importance or significance of an alteration to the image as a whole: Does the
alteration distance the image from its implication of authenticity? Critics
might debate whether the fictional aspect of *Rolling Stone*'s Don Johnson
cover was substantial or trivial, but regarding the *Newsday* image there can
be no doubt: The fiction was *the essence of the image*. The skaters' juxtaposition was the whole point of the "photo," rather than a mere enhancement
or even an "alteration" (alterations are made to existing objects; the *Newsday* image did not exist at all until separate photos were joined). The result
was a mismatch between implied and actual authenticity. Given its potential
for misleading readers in fundamental ways, such a manipulation, if defensible at all, would seem to carry a heavier obligation of disclosure.

The "content vs. enhancement" distinction can also come into play here.
Photographer Art Wolfe (himself criticized for his digitally altered
"wildlife" images) reported to Kenneth Brower the attitudes of photographers attending a September 1997 ethics conference hosted by the National

> Don't give a false impression . . . The only thing we have to avoid is misleading readers through a "created reality". . . . we ran an image of chimps in a library, suggesting that old saying about how enough chimps with typewriters working long enough would eventually reproduce Shakespeare. There was no possible connection to reality, and yet we went so far as to write a separate piece informing readers about how we created the image. Disclosure is the key.
>
> — Bill Allen, National Geographic[5]

Museum of Wildlife Art in Jackson Hole, Wyoming: "I think the rest of the photographers at Jackson Hole thought that [labeling] was the most appropriate way of presenting the work. They also felt that digital *enhancement*—darkening of sky, say, and other things that had been done in the past by printing techniques in the darkroom—need not be labeled."[6]

Another consideration is the commercial significance of the fiction. Few people based their decision to purchase the Don Johnson *Rolling Stone* on the fact that its cover was altered. That is, few passersby bought that issue because the picture lacked a handgun. But *Newsday*'s front-page, large-format Harding/Kerrigan composite—complete with sensational headline—provided the issue's chief selling point, compounding its potential for duping readers. The photo seemed to convey, "Here's the update you've been waiting for." But the fine print revealed that the photo did not mean what it said after all. Given the higher commercial stakes, such a manipulation would seem to increase obligations of disclosure—not to mention calling into question whether the image is defensible at all.

VISUAL SPECULATION

Newsday's Harding/Kerrigan cover might be described as visual speculation—here's how the skaters might look when and if they meet. But consider an analogy drawn from the rules and conventions of journalistic text: Would readers tolerate a newspaper headline announcing "President Admits Election Fraud" accompanied by a fine-print disclaimer that it was mere speculation about what *might* occur? Should undisclosed visual speculation be allowed in contexts in which undisclosed written speculation would be vehemently forbidden? (Regarding the comparison of altering photos to altering quotes, see Chapter 11.)

Of course, if speculation is identified as such, it may be ethical—in photos as well as in text. In 1994 a Hasidic rabbi was sent to prison in New York. The state mandates that inmates be photographed clean shaven, but the rabbi's religion dictates that he not shave. A photo of the bearded rabbi was digitally retouched so as to "remove" the beard, and the state accepted the image as a legitimate document.[7] All sorts of manipulations may be appropriate when viewers know what they're viewing.

LOCATION OF DISCLOSURES

Photo credits typically run sideways up the border of the image, or appear in the gutter or on another page altogether. Is such positioning good enough for a disclosure of "essence of the image" photofiction? In a word, no.

Most readers do not care who took most photos. A credit line in some out-of-the-way place may be adequate to acknowledge the photographer, or to inform a reader who wants to identify the photographer and knows where to look. But if we assume that most readers do care if a purportedly journalistic image is in fact fictional, particularly in an "essence of the image" case, it calls for a label appropriate not only in its wording but also in its prominence.

For example, if the image takes a caption, the disclosure could come at the end of it, in the same point size: *Computer photofiction by Imaginary Image, Inc.* If there's no caption per se, then the disclosure itself could fill the caption's space. Or the disclosure could be worked into the caption, as in an example from *The Toledo Blade* in which an apparently crowded baseball stadium was pictured the day before it actually opened: "Cleveland's Jacobs Field. A computer enhancement shows how it may look for the baseball opener tomorrow." In another example, the October 2001 *Road & Track* magazine pictured a 2004–2005 Camaro. The caption: "This computer-generated image is based on. . . ." (For a similar example, see Figure 16.2.)

Another example of a "caption disclosure" is included in an article in the October 1998 issue of *GQ*, in which a man who had undergone a sex change operation is pictured. His earlier and later incarnations appear as a

---

Brill's Content's Photo Guidelines

At <u>Brill's Content</u> magazine, the published photo guidelines include the following:

1. Photos used should reflect the truth.
2. Retouching should be done only to alter minor points about the photo and should never be done to alter facts or change anyone's appearance.
3. Any changes in a picture are to be clearly noted in the picture caption.

It is this third point that lets you, the consumer, decide whether you can trust what you see and read in <u>Brill's Content</u>.[8]

Is it real? That's a question that could kill journalism.
—Ted Pease, <u>Logan Herald Journal</u>[9]

couple, arm in arm. The photolike illustration is remarkable, even stunning, and its prominent caption is a model of straightforwardness. It begins, "In this manipulated, composite image. . . ."

"BATTERED NICOLE"

Are some examples of photofiction so objectionable that *no* amount of disclosure could get the publication off the ethical hook? *National Enquirer*'s January 3, 1995, issue pictured a shocking photo of a battered and bruised Nicole Brown Simpson, O.J. Simpson's slain wife. The original photo was rather ordinary and had previously appeared, apparently unretouched, on *Newsweek*'s July 4, 1994, cover. Bruises and welts were added by *National Enquirer*'s digital retouchers.

FIGURE 16.2.   A "photograph" of a future event sounds like an impossibility, but technology now allows predictions or speculations to be rendered in photorealistic images. In 2001, <u>Road & Track</u> published this picture of a car to be manufactured in different incarnations in 2003 and 2004. Created by Brenda Priddy & Co., it was accompanied by an admirably straightforward caption: "This computer-enhanced photo of Opel's 2003 Astra shows the radical shape that the 2004 Chevrolet Cavalier will take on. . . ."

> Is this what newspapers should be doing? Whether there's an icon there or not, it's still manipulation. I don't think that a label would transform the fact of it.
>
> —Janet Froelich, <u>The New York Times Magazine</u>, regarding <u>Newsday</u>'s Harding/Kerrigan image[10]

On the *National Enquirer* cover, a disclosure in the lower right corner said "computer re-creation." Did that render the manipulation acceptable? Photojournalist, educator, and author Ken Kobre saw the publication at a grocery store. He wrote:

> Like most of us who stare but don't buy, I paid for my groceries and left without a copy of the *Enquirer*. The shocking picture came up in conversation later, however, and it was only then that someone referred to the smaller type below the picture. . . . Supposedly sensitive to faked pictures and computer manipulation, I had somehow been so shocked by the sight of the murder victim's bruised face that I had . . . missed the fact that the picture was doctored.[11]

PRIMING THE PUBLIC

Prior to the "Battered Nicole" story, it had been widely reported that the murder victim's sister had claimed to have taken photos of Nicole to document her beating by O.J. Simpson, that authorities had removed certain objects from Nicole's safe deposit box and that her sister had then claimed that these objects likely included her photos. Finally, it was no secret that *National Enquirer* was offering money to figures in the case for rights to their stories—and presumably for their photos as well. Wouldn't these developments set up or prime the public for the appearance of photos that looked much like the "Battered Nicole" cover? Wouldn't previous media coverage of actual facts make the "photo" seem plausible, especially at first glance? How might such circumstances affect the ethics of the image?

SUMMARY

Setting off some words in italics is a common alteration to quotations in journalistic text, either to capture a speaker's or a quoted writer's own emphasis, or to highlight some aspect of the spoken or written quote. In the latter case, such treatments are typically accompanied by the words "emphasis added." This simple phrase is a model of disclosure: Readers cannot miss it because it is as prominent as the quote itself, and they understand it because it unambiguously specifies the nature of the treatment.

Like disclosures of text alterations, effective disclosures of image alterations must be specific, and, in some cases, prominent. The required level of prominence increases with the image's potential to mislead, as when any of the following circumstances applies:

- The fiction provides the essence of the image (as opposed to mere enhancement).
- The image is the publication's chief selling point.
- The public has been conditioned by reports of actual events to interpret the fiction as reality.

EXPLORATIONS

1. Bring to class examples of manipulated photography identified with a label ("photo-illustration," "digitally altered," etc.). This time, examine the location and prominence of the label or disclosure—in the caption, along the side of the image, on a different page, etc. How many different levels of prominence can you find? In each case, how do the type of publication, the type of image, and the type of alteration seem to relate to the disclosure's level of prominence?

2. How does a publication's reputation affect its obligations regarding disclosure of altered photography, if at all? For example, consider *Spy*'s reputation for flagrant satire, as well as its history of featuring composite cover photos.

3. Regarding *National Enquirer*'s "Battered Nicole" cover, did you decide the photo alteration was ethical or unethical? Would your decision depend not only on the presence or the actual wording of the disclosure ("computer re-creation") but also on its prominence? To render the manipulation acceptable, would a fine-print disclosure—something many passers-by would miss altogether—be adequate? Or would the disclosure have to be so prominent (perhaps different words in bigger type and bright colors) as to constitute one of the cover's major graphic elements? Might this be a case where the disclosure would have to be *so* prominent that it would effectively destroy the visual integrity or commercial appeal of the cover? Might this be a case where *no* amount of disclosure could offset the unethical aspects of the alteration?

4. In Chapter 5 ("Rationales, Excuses, and Justifications for Staging and Manipulating Photos"), we considered the argument that because *National Enquirer* or similar tabloids are known for sensational stories their photo alterations are not significant. Then again, in recent years *National Enquirer* has made efforts to increase its credibility (during the very period when traditional news publications have been accused of "tabloidization"—in general becoming

more like *National Enquirer*). In Chapter 5 we asked, what about a tabloid's impact on passers-by who absorb a cover's message without seeing disclaimers, or without considering the publication's reputation, or without even noticing its name? Discuss those issues here in relation to the Battered Nicole cover.

5. In judging the ethics of the composite Harding/Kerrigan image on *Newsday*'s cover, observers considered not only the disclaimer in the fine-print caption but also other clues that might have tipped off viewers that the "pictured" event had not yet happened (one example: the future tense of the subhead—"Tonya, Nancy to Meet at Practice"—might have indicated that the meeting had yet to occur; then again, would readers make the connection?). But aside from cover type, captions, and disclaimers, did the mere appearance of what seemed to be a real photo on the front page of a real newspaper imply that it portrayed a real event? How does your answer tie in to our previous discussion of magazine covers and book covers and their implied levels of authenticity (see Chapter 10)?

6. Regarding the Harding/Kerrigan *Newsday* cover image, consider the broader environment of public awareness into which the image was introduced, and how news accounts might have predisposed viewers to make certain assumptions upon seeing it. Given media coverage of the upcoming Kerrigan/Harding meeting, didn't the image seem to be a logical update, conforming to publicized facts and actual events?

ENDNOTES

1. Professor Gissler teaches at the Columbia University Graduate School of Journalism; quoted in G. Bruce Knecht, "At *USA Today*, a Staged Photo Isn't Good News," *The Wall Street Journal* (August 22, 1996): B7.
2. J. D. Lasica, "Photographs That Lie: The Ethical Dilemma of Digital Retouching," *Washington Journalism Review* (June 1989): 25; see also, George Tuck, "Integrity of Photograph: An Issue in State-of-the-Art Digital-Imaging Systems," *1987 Associated Press Managing Editors Photo & Graphics Report*, 14.
3. From an e-mail correspondence with the author, fall 1998.
4. William Glaberson, "*Newsday* Imagines an Event, and Sets Off a Debate," *The New York Times* (February 17, 1994): A12.
5. From an e-mail correspondence with the author, fall 1998.
6. Kenneth Brower, "Photography in the Age of Falsification," *Atlantic Monthly* (May 1998): 107.
7. George James, "Computer Replaces Razor for Rabbi's Prison Picture," *The New York Times* (December 29, 1994): A13.
8. Bill Kovach, "Report from the Ombudsman," *Brill's Content* (November 1998): 31.
9. Ted Pease, "Putting the Bite on Press Ethics," *Logan Herald Journal*, Logan, UT (December 7, 1997): 33.
10. Janet Abrams, "Little Photoshop of Horrors: The Ethics of Manipulating Journalistic Imagery," *Print* (November/December 1995): 28.
11. Ken Kobre, "The Long Tradition of Doctoring Photos," *Visual Communication Quarterly* (Spring 1995): 14–15.

Chapter 17

Cosmetic Retouching

Skin Deep?

Airbrushing age off women's faces has the same political echo that would resound if all positive images of blacks were routinely lightened. That would be making the same value judgment about blackness that this tampering makes about the value of the female life: that less is more. To airbrush age off a woman's face is to erase women's identity, power, and history.

—Naomi Wolf, *The Beauty Myth*[1]

ADDRESSING COSMETIC RETOUCHING —WHY BOTHER?

Given that many readers recognize the virtually universal practice of retouching photos in fashion/beauty magazines, those publications are excluded from the conception of the nonfiction photographic environment presented in Chapter 10. Why bother? After all, these publications are not hard news; most or all of their photos are clearly posed set-ups that probably will not fool anyone. Touched-up portraits are as old as photography and seem trivial compared to falsifications of political events, battlefield scenes, and so on, and besides, these magazines are not about to stop retouching their photos in any case.

All these statements are true. Nevertheless, we will briefly examine the topic here—not because fashion, glamour, and beauty magazines should be held to photojournalistic standards, but for other reasons:

- Retouching is hardly confined to *Vogue, Allure*, and magazines of that ilk. It occurs in a broad range of contexts, including purportedly journalistic media.
- While the term "cosmetic" connotes trivial, superficial alterations, image manipulation in fashion magazines includes much more drastic examples, such as a *Harper's Bazaar* cover "photo" of Princess Caroline of Monaco that was actually a composite of images of skin, hair, face, and torso from four different photographs.[2] As we will see, sometimes the manipulation is so extreme as to constitute visual fiction.

- The practice of cosmetic retouching is applied to images not only of fashion models and entertainment celebrities, but also those of sports stars, political figures, "ordinary" citizens, and others.
- For many observers, the most insidious aspect of the practice is not that it fails to meet photojournalistic standards but that taken cumulatively it promotes harmful stereotypes, particularly of women.
- Finally, the more society is inundated with photofiction of all kinds, from all sources, the weaker the foundation of photocredibility in any context, even journalism, becomes.

Bad Hair Day

A truly cosmetic touch-up to remove a pimple or to correct some other temporary "imperfection" seems harmless to many professionals and probably to many readers as well, at least in contexts other than hard news. One could argue that such enhancements make the subject look *more* like he or she does most of the time, by "correcting" unrepresentative details.

Aside from perceived commercial disadvantages, it is unfair and even misleading, the argument goes, to capture for all time (or at least to publicize for a while) an image of someone who's having a bad hair day, or whose sleep-deprived eyes happen to be bloodshot at the moment the shutter is clicked, or whose jet lag has added a temporary facial line or two. If these sorts of things can be fixed with a hairbrush or eyedrops or makeup anyway, why not fix them in the darkroom or on the computer?

But What about the Viewfinder Test?

Discounting the point of view expressed previously, some say that arguments about whether facial "imperfections" are temporary or permanent are irrelevant. Nonfiction photography promises viewers that they see what the camera saw at the time the camera saw it—not what it *might* have seen on a different day or under more ideal circumstances.

Once again, this is a judgment call. Decision makers might ask: Given our publication's mission and our responsibility to our readers, what level of authenticity is implied by our photography's content and context? Does it meet that standard?

EVEN NEWS MAGAZINES DO IT (SOMETIMES)

In television advertising we are used to unreal images—cola-guzzling polar bears, wisecracking bayou bullfrogs, a skyboarding Gen X'er who pops open his Pepsi and treats a migrating goose to a midair refueling. Print advertising "photos" are often just as phony, whether touched up, assembled from composites, or created from scratch.

What about touch-ups in journalistic photos, including magazine covers or pictures accompanying feature articles? Many readers may know that images of fashion models are routinely touched up (as *The New York Times* put it, "making the subjects look freakishly flawless").[3] But do they know that images of celebrities and even "ordinary" citizens are often manipulated as well, not only to remove blemishes and facial lines but also to brighten eyes; to whiten, straighten, or replace teeth; to change clothing; even to sculpt physiques? Do they know that these manipulations have appeared not only in "beauty books" but also in more general consumer publications such as *TV Guide* and *Ladies' Home Journal*; in magazines with distinguished literary traditions such as *Esquire* and *Rolling Stone*; even in news magazines such as *Newsweek*?

There is little research addressing readers' awareness of retouching,[4] but while most people might not be surprised to learn that fashion and celebrity photos are typically touched up, they would likely be surprised indeed to learn how drastic some manipulations are, and how often they appear in supposedly nonfiction contexts.

Tori Spelling in Details

A profile of *Beverly Hills 90210* actress Tori Spelling appeared in the ostensibly journalistic *Details* magazine along with a photo that was reprinted on the July/August 1997 cover of the professionally oriented *American Photo* (Figure 17.1). According to the *Chicago Tribune*, the actress received a body makeover accomplished with computers and airbrushing: A facial blemish or blemishes were removed, her lips were made fuller, her cleavage was increased, the visibility of her nipples (under her clothing) was enhanced, her waist was decreased, and her legs were lengthened. Although these alterations went beyond the routine cosmetic touch-ups readers may accept, there was no disclosure.[5]

Michelle Pfeiffer in Esquire

Michelle Pfeiffer is regularly called one of the most beautiful actresses in Hollywood, but her studio photo did not look quite good enough for *Esquire*'s December 1990 cover. The invoice for $1,525 worth of retouching included dozens of items, not only for "clean up complexion, soften eye lines, soften smile line, add color to lips, . . . remove neck lines, soften line under ear lobe," and so on, but also for "trim chin" and "add forehead."[6] (Ironically, the magazine's cover type suggested, "What Michelle Pfeiffer Needs . . . Is Absolutely Nothing.")

> I worry about an entire generation of kids growing up thinking of the augmented, implanted breast as the norm. Real breasts may begin to look ugly or grotesque to them.
>
> —Susan Bordo, University of Kentucky[7]

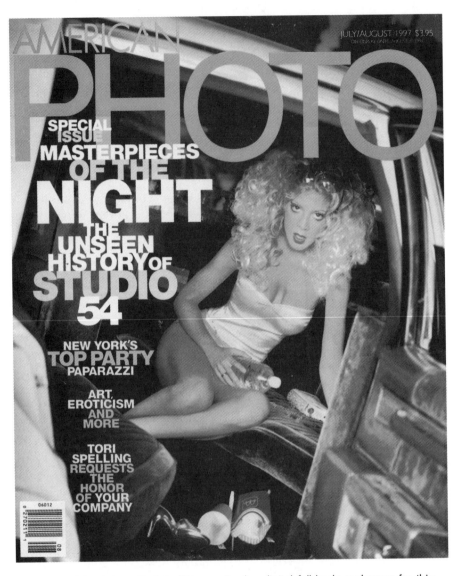

FIGURE 17.1. Actress Tori Spelling received a digital full-body makeover for this "photo," raising questions about the line between "cosmetic" retouching and raw fiction.

Demi Moore on the Cover of <u>Rolling Stone</u>

Given *Rolling Stone*'s award-winning journalism and editorial mix of music, fashion, politics, and so on, what is the implication of authenticity of its cover photo of actress Demi Moore (February 9, 1995)? In one unrepresentative, unscientific sample, several students offered such comments as, "Boy, she looks athletic and fit for someone who's had three children. She's in shape!" A young mother said, "I had just had my child when I saw that picture, and somehow it made me feel terrible, not so much her beauty,

> Fashion magazines and other magazines have improved or thought they improved pictures forever. . . . you can't assume a fashion photo is a U.P.I. picture of a war zone.
> —Patrick McCarthy, Fairchild Publications[8]

which is fine, but I knew my body would never look like that." Another student: "That's what you can do if you have a home gym and a personal trainer and you work out every day. Look at that stomach!" That stomach, or the image of it, was tightened, de-wrinkled, and de-blemished by graphic artists. Although the credit line included separate credits for the photo, makeup, styling, and hair, there was no mention of the tummy job.

CUMULATIVE EFFECTS AND STEREOTYPES

A particularly elusive aspect of context entails the *frequency* of alterations and their cumulative effects. People who defend such "minor touch-ups" as removing blemishes or facial lines from models' faces contend that they do not change a photo's fundamental meaning, and that readers probably know of such alterations (or would not be shocked to learn of them) and are not misled by them. They may also assert that fashion or beauty photos are not news, and thus carry little or no implications of veracity.

On the other hand, critics argue that for decades the public has been inundated with countless unreal or idealized images of women, and the effects are damaging to society: They diminish the self-esteem of impressionable readers (including some who realize that many such photos are retouched),[9] reinforce harmful stereotypes, and objectify women. In other words, the argument goes, such "technical enhancements" are not minor at all, especially when considered cumulatively. They are alterations to photographic content that seem particularly hypocritical given women's magazines' earnest pledges that they support and empower their readers.

IF THE TEXT IS NONFICTION, WHY NOT THE IMAGES?

Magazines in general-interest, self-help, lifestyle, outdoor, and other consumer categories may not purport to be hard-news or strictly photojournalistic publications. But unless otherwise informed, readers perceive their content to be nonfiction. Such magazines' articles on travel, sports, gardening, personal finance, fitness, and any number of topics carry substantial implications of authenticity and are presumed to meet basic journalistic standards of accuracy.

In this sense, at least, such publications are not much different from news magazines or newspapers: The text may appear in alternatives to the "inverted pyramid" (a traditional story structure in newspapers), and it may reflect more of the writer's own point of view than in hard-news accounts, but the articles are supposed to be true. Fiction masquerading as nonfiction would be ethically intolerable. Why should the photos accompanying those same articles be held to a different standard?

ONE MAGAZINE, SEVERAL STANDARDS?

General-interest magazines by definition address several subtopics. While *Esquire, Rolling Stone, Playboy*, and others may win numerous awards for reporting or journalism, they also cover travel, fashion, celebrity profiles, and other areas in which posed photos, altered photos, or unidentified "photo illustrations" are more acceptable. This editorial mix makes it all the more difficult to establish consistent standards. Certainly, if magazines with the literary history and journalistic achievements of *Rolling Stone* and *Esquire* are willing to extensively "touch up" their photos, it is naive to expect other celebrity-oriented media to discontinue the practice.

Still, as we learned in Chapter 7, in a nonfiction environment even "soft feature" photos carry at least some implication of veracity. If publications applied to images the same standards of authenticity and disclosure they apply to text, readers would be better served, the profession would be held in higher regard, and photocredibility would be more secure.

A SLIDING SCALE

Professionals who wish to help preserve photocredibility might consider the following sliding scale, which they can adapt to their own perceived responsibilities and standards:

- Allow no touch-ups at all in news accounts. Newspapers and news magazines, at least, should abide by this standard.
- Confine any touch-ups to correcting temporary "imperfections" such as blemishes. This less-rigorous standard might be embraced by serious, responsible, but less photojournalistic publications.
- Avoid changes to body proportions and other drastic manipulations except in satire or other obvious photofiction—extreme manipulations seem inexcusable even at publications with only nominal pretensions of journalistic standards. Even celebrity oriented magazines should avoid bamboozling their readers, although, admittedly, many of them find themselves in deep holes of their own digging, having surrendered photo approval or some other measure of editorial control in exchange for access to celebrities whose (often touched-up) faces are considered surefire guarantees of newsstand success.

This censorship [airbrushing away signs of aging] extends beyond women's magazines to any image of an older woman: Bob Ciano, once art director of <u>Life</u> magazine, says that "no picture of a woman goes unretouched . . . even a well-known [older] woman who doesn't want to be retouched . . . we still persist in trying to make her look like she's in her fifties." The effect of this censorship of a third of the female life span is clear to [women's magazine editor Dalma] Heyn: "By now readers have no idea what a real woman's 60-year-old face looks like in print."

—Naomi Wolfe, <u>The Beauty Myth</u>[10]

VIRTUALLY IMPOSSIBLE STANDARDS

The creation of what *The New York Times* in May 2001 called "cyberbabes" raises a host of issues. Although their animated movements sometimes entail the preliminary filming of real actors, these "models" and "starlets" exist only in the digital realm. John Casablancas was the founder of the prestigious Elite Model Management agency. He left Elite to found Illusion 2K, a company that supervises the careers of cyber models. Referring to one of the stars in his new stable, he said, "Webbie can eat nothing and keep her curves . . . she will never get a pimple or ask for a raise. Sometimes I wish all models were virtual."

However manageable Webbie and her cyber sidekicks may be, their existence (if one can call it that) increases the already sizeable gap between celebrities and the real-life viewers who may look to them as standard setters. Such idealized digital creations are literally unrealistic role models for females already held to standards that are, for most, all but impossible to attain. Suzanna Walters, director of feminist studies at Georgetown University, calls them "the postmodern equivalent of the mail-order bride . . . compliant creatures created for one's pleasure, another example of the female as object."[11]

SUMMARY

Regardless of the methods involved, "improving" a subject's appearance is one of the most perplexing topics addressed in this book. The term "cosmetic" suggests a certain superficiality or insignificance, or that the practice is confined to a category of media imagery in which journalistic standards are elastic if not altogether absent. And yet the practice poses a troubling mismatch between supposedly nonfiction text and the manipulated imagery that sometimes accompanies it. The practice is occasionally taken to extremes, extends far beyond mainstream fashion magazines, and may further weaken the shaky foundation of photocredibility in several contexts.

Art directors will probably continue touching-up celebrity images in general interest magazines and certainly images of models in fashion magazines. Many of them have manipulated so many photos so drastically for so long that sudden jolts of journalistic sensibility are unlikely. Still, it is reasonable to demand of publications presenting articles on news, nature, travel, sports, and any other nonfiction topic that they abandon the dubious rationalization that readers who expect truth in text would accept substantial, undisclosed fiction in accompanying images.

EXPLORATIONS

1. Reconsider the Tori Spelling photo discussed in this chapter (Figure 17.1). Did the alterations change the photo's content? Did they change its meaning, fictionalize the image, or mislead readers? Did they cross the line from ethical to unethical? If so, which of the alterations are unacceptable? Can you state a guideline or standard that separates the acceptable and unacceptable alterations? Do readers have much of an expectation of authenticity in consumer magazine photos that accompany purportedly truthful text?

2. *Esquire*'s alterations to the photo of Michelle Pfeiffer raise the issue of quantity versus quality. It was the quality of the alterations (altered body proportions, etc.) that made the Tori Spelling photo objectionable to some observers, while the Pfeiffer alterations seem trivial by comparison—and yet there were so many of them. Is there some point at which "cosmetic touch ups" become so numerous that their cumulative effect rivals the lengthened legs and the tucked waists of radical (if digital) surgeries?

3. In regard to fashion and beauty photos, some people argue that removing a blemish or a facial line is no big deal. Others assert that the constant "improvement" of women's faces and bodies affects photography's impact, its meaning. Even if one particular alteration to one particular photo seems trivial, the long-term consequences of mass-media stereotypes are significant indeed.

   Does either view reflect your opinion? Even if we exclude fashion and beauty imagery from our discussion of nonfiction photography, shouldn't responsible visual communicators ask themselves whether so-called trivial alterations might contribute to harmful stereotypes that promote (even unintentionally) sexism, ageism, racism or other prejudices?

ENDNOTES

1. Naomi Wolf, *The Beauty Myth: How Images of Beauty Are Used against Women* (New York: Morrow, 1991), 83.
2. Amy M. Spindler, "Making the Camera Lie, Digitally and Often," *The New York Times* (June 17, 1997): B8.
3. Spindler, B8.
4. See Readers' Awareness of Retouching, Chapter 9.
5. *Chicago Tribune* (August 17, 1993): A14.
6. Cosmetic Perjury column, "What Michelle Pfeiffer Needs," *Adbusters Quarterly* (Summer 1995): 9.
7. Quoted in Michelle Stacy, "The Naked Truth: Behind the New Eroticism," *American Photo* (September/October 1999): 38. Professor Bordo is the author of *The Male Body: A New Look at Men in Public and in Private* (New York: Farrar, Straus, and Giroux, 1999).
8. Patrick McCarthy is the chairman and editorial director of Fairchild Publications, owners of *Los Angeles Magazine, Women's Wear Daily* and *W* magazines; quoted in Spindler, B8.
9. But see Erica Goode (*The New York Times*), "Study: Most girls unaffected by thin images," *The Register-Guard*, Eugene, OR, August 30, 1999, 3D. Professors at Stanford, the University of Texas and Brigham Young conducted a study of 219 teenaged girls over a 20-month period. Half of the girls read *Seventeen* magazine; half did not. Most of the girls who read the publication were unaffected by its images of ultra-thin models, but "girls who were already vulnerable showed more dieting, body dissatisfaction, anxiety and bulimic symptoms" than members of the other group.
10. Wolf, 82–83.
11. Ruth La Ferla, "Perfect Model, Gorgeous, No Complaints, Made of Pixels," *The New York Times* (May 7, 2001): B8.

Chapter 18

Applying the Guidelines
Case Studies

A lot has changed in the business and art of photography during the past two decades . . . but still photography is, we feel, more important than ever. Photographs are emotionally enduring; indeed, photojournalism has come to serve as a powerful repository of history, a collective modern memory.

—*American Photo*[1]

RECAPPING THE PHOTO-ASSESSMENT STEPS

Although misleading photos can result from actions and decisions occurring at any number of stages, the following guidelines focus on post-exposure processing. If alterations to a mass-media photograph raise doubts about its appropriateness or ethics, here is a recommended sequence of questions to ask:

1. Will the image appear in a nonfiction photographic environment, as broadly defined in Chapter 10?
2. If so, is the image an example of post-exposure photofiction, as defined in Chapter 12? Apply the viewfinder test and nonfiction photography's process test (Chapter 13).
3. If indeed we face the conflict of a photofictional image in a nonfiction environment, is the image's fiction so obvious that readers are not likely to be misled? Use the tests of technical credibility and obvious implausibility (Chapter 14). Obvious photofiction could include visual satire, an image of an object or event that could not exist in the physical world, or some other type of non-photojournalistic illustration or "photo-cartoon." If the photo is obviously implausible, or its technical incoherence gives away the manipulation, there may be little obligation to disclose it aside from crediting digital artists or other contributors.
4. What is the image's implication of authenticity? Throughout this book, what distinctions did you make between altering the bathing

suit on the cover of the lifestyle magazine and altering the covers of news magazines or photos in newspapers? Where did you draw the line? Considering all aspects of context, is disclosure required in the case at hand? If so, it should be straightforward (Chapter 15) and appropriately prominent (Chapter 16). One useful guideline is the essence of the image test (Chapter 16).

THREE QUESTIONS, ONE ISSUE

The protocol's first four tests—viewfinder, process, technical credibility, and obvious implausibility—illuminate a crucial issue:

- Has a presumably nonfiction mass-media image been fictionalized in some way that is not immediately obvious?
- Does the image fall outside the reader's QER?
- Does it fail to meet the implied authenticity established by its context?

However we phrase the question, if the answer is yes, publication of the image—or failure to disclose its manipulation—is a breach of faith, a violation of the public trust that risks a loss of credibility.

The following hypothetical cases provide opportunities to apply the guidelines for yourself.

CASE STUDY: HURRICANE SURVIVORS

Assume that a devastating hurricane has struck a coastal town. The day after the hurricane hit, a news photographer arrives on the scene.

Hurricane Survivors, Round One

Scenario 1: The news photographer surveys the scene, then assembles a local family—father, mother, son and daughter, plus the family dog. The photographer wishes to pose them in front of their destroyed home, but the structure has slid off a cliff and is out of view. The photographer instead poses the family in front of a neighbor's destroyed home.

Scenario 2: The same as Scenario 1, except the neighbor's destroyed home is photographed separately. With computer technology, the photo of the home (including sky, trees, and the rest of the background) is "dropped in" behind the family photo.

Scenario 3: The same as Scenario 2, except the family is photographed in the photographer's studio. On a computer, their photo is combined with the background shot of the neighbor's house.

The three resulting images appear identical. For each scenario, assume the following facts: The photo runs in a daily newspaper with the caption "In the wake of yesterday's hurricane, many families lost their homes." The editor considers the photo misleading and threatens to fire the photographer.

The photographer argues that the family in the photo did in fact lose their home; the addition of the destroyed structure makes the photo not only more dramatic but also more representative of the scene, not less; and the caption is 100% true.

Regarding the versions that combine photos on a computer, the photographer argues that what matters is the veracity of the final image, not the process. In other words, if the results look the same, it makes no difference whether the process entailed one original photo or two.

What do you think? Does each photo actually "mean" what it seems to "say"? That is, does it picture what typical viewers would conclude it pictures? What is each photo's implication of authenticity? Does it pass the viewfinder test or the process test? Is it legitimate? If not, would some sort of disclaimer or label make it legitimate? Or would a sufficiently explanatory caption render the photo unwieldy or otherwise impractical?

Can the ethics of each example be determined apart from its context? For instance, can an ethical judgment be made without analyzing the precise meaning and implications of the caption?

Hurricane Survivors, Round Two

Scenario 4: The day after a devastating hurricane strikes a coastal town, a news photographer assembles several survivors at the scene—a woman, a man, a young boy, and a young girl, all of whom are photogenic but none of whom are related. The photographer adds her own dog to the group, poses them all in front of a destroyed home that had belonged to someone not among the group, and clicks the shutter.

Scenario 5: At the scene, the photographer takes separate photos of four unrelated hurricane victims, her own dog, and a home destroyed in the hurricane. The six photos are combined on a computer. The result looks like the four people and the dog are posed together in front of a destroyed home.

We are winning the small battles, but the war is over and we have lost. There is a definite paradigm shift in our understanding of photography. . . . A photograph used to be a solid piece of paper with silver deposits on it that, once made, could not be changed — at least not without it being obvious. It seemed to be a permanent thing. However, images in computers are totally changeable, liquid, whatever you want them to be. In ads, art, whatever, I have no problem with this, but it is killing documentary photojournalism. People do not trust any image, and rightly so.

— John Long, former president, NPPA[2]

Scenario 6: The same as Scenario 5, except the people and the dog are photographed in a studio.

For each scenario, assume these facts: The photo runs in a daily newspaper with the caption "In the wake of yesterday's hurricane, many families lost their homes." The editor considers the photo misleading and threatens to fire the photographer, who argues that the photo accurately typifies the experience of hurricane survivors, and the caption is 100% true.

For convenience and discussion purposes, a synopsis of all six scenarios appears below.

Synopsis: Hurricane Survivors, Rounds One and Two

1. Single photo at scene; actual family; neighbor's home
2. Same, except the home is photographed separately and "dropped in"
3. Same as Scenario 2, except family photographed in studio; photos combined on computer
4. Single photo at scene; unrelated survivors and photographer's dog; someone else's home
5. Six photos at scene; unrelated survivors plus dog and someone else's home; computer-composited
6. Five photos in studio; unrelated survivors plus dog; computer-composited with photo of someone else's home.

One Possible Assessment. Even if the photo appeared in a context that is only nominally journalistic, anything other than full disclosure would violate the reader's Qualified Expectation of Reality. The first scenario would be acceptable if the caption explained that the home in the background belonged

> I don't believe photography's "credibility" is on the ropes. We still use it to document our lives, no matter how prosaic or predictable, and we turn to it constantly to take us places we've never been via <u>National Geographic</u>, to catch a glimpse of a celebrity in <u>Rolling Stone</u>, to rerun our experience of a football game in the sports section of the local paper. Readers aren't scratching chins or wondering if the photography was retouched or posed. I'm not talking about the "I was sucked into a roaring jet engine but lived" tabloid mentality (that's entertainment anyway), but rather the local newspapers and wide array of magazines people use to connect with their communities and interests. I believe average readers know enough about manipulation and its potential for misuse to bring fairly sensitive antennae to their judgment about what they see.
>
> — Bill Ryan, University of Oregon[3]

to a neighbor. The details of all other scenarios would have to be disclosed in captions, which would likely make them unwieldy in journalistic environments. The images in Scenarios 2 through 6 could be used in nonjournalistic contexts such as advertisements or public safety brochures. Do you agree?

The Importance of Process. The argument that content matters more than process seems convincing on its face. Even a computer composite may pass the viewfinder test if the images are combined to re-create what the photographer actually saw. But such procedures violate the reader's Qualified Expectation of Reality as it relates to journalistic process, which is another way of saying they violate typical notions of what a photograph really is. We "take" pictures. Images are "captured." The implied promise of a nonfiction photo is not merely "this event or scene could have happened," but, rather, "this event or scene did happen; we 'caught' it on film."

This promise acknowledges photography's subjectivity and many qualifications, but maintains that the image has not been altered in a misleading way. Unless informed otherwise, typical readers will likely assume that journalistic photos are just that—photos—rather than composites of separate images. Although a composite that faithfully re-creates an actual scene may be less problematic than raw fiction, don't readers depend on journalistic photographers to capture or at least to reflect reality, rather than to reconstruct it?

Hurricane Survivors, Round Three

The day after a devastating hurricane strikes a coastal town, a news photographer spies a house, its windows covered with plywood. After ascertaining that the plywood had been nailed up by the homeowners, she asks the homeowners to lift and position plywood in front of a window of their home in a reasonably faithful re-creation of their earlier activity. The photographer takes pictures, one of which runs in a daily newspaper with the caption "The Smith family hurriedly protects their home's windows with plywood in anticipation of the next storm." The photographer defends the photo and caption by saying "it happened."

Does the photo mean what it seems to say? Is it ethical? Given its content—and the precise wording of its caption—does it picture what typical viewers would conclude it pictures? Does it meet its implication of authenticity? If the photo is unethical, or marginally ethical, would a different caption make it more ethical? Or would a sufficiently explanatory caption render the photo unwieldy or otherwise impractical?

The absence of pictures would help make historians mute and the world deaf.

— Norman Salsitz, <u>A Harvest of Jewish Memories</u>[4]

Why Not Just Call It a Portrait?

Could the photo qualify as a portrait, with the portrait's greater allowance for posing? Photojournalist Larry Coyne addressed similar issues in the July/August 1995 *Viewpoint* [Scripps Howard News]:

> "This gets into a gray area: What constitutes a portrait? Can we ask someone to do something for us (paint the picture, paint the house, mow the yard, etc.), call it a portrait, and then ethically justify the image for publication in a newspaper? No, it must be *obvious to the reader* that a portrait is not the documentation of a "real" moment, and that the subject is aware he is having his picture made. This can be achieved in numerous ways, the simplest being that the subject is looking at the camera."

Do you agree? Mr. Coyne referred to newspapers. Should standards be different for news magazines or general-interest magazines?

CASE STUDY: PRESIDENTIAL PORTRAIT

Consider a hypothetical photo of the president of the United States. Let us imagine the president is a married man with a young daughter, a second grader. Suppose he wants a picture of himself and his child, so he summons the White House photographer. Consider four scenarios.

In the first, the photographer prints up a large batch of photos from existing negatives and presents them to the president as options; in some of them, the president and his daughter are smiling or laughing.

In the second scenario, existing photos are rejected because the daughter invariably looks unhappy or distracted, so the photographer takes new photos. Now suppose the president is a cold and remote parent with little interest in the child. In fact, he and she dislike each other; she is even afraid of him at times. She has to be cajoled into posing for the session and in most of the frames looks unhappy. The photographer has to shoot four rolls of film before finally capturing an acceptable image in which the daughter appears to be smiling.

In the third scenario, a photo of the president and his daughter is digitized; the daughter's face is manipulated with software until she appears to be smiling.

In the fourth scenario, two photos are selected: one of the smiling president holding the family dog on his lap, and one of the smiling daughter playing with her best friend. The images are Photoshopped, with the daughter replacing the dog on the president's lap.

Presidential Portrait, Questions

Assume the resulting images are the same in every case, as is the caption: "The president with his daughter at home in the White House." In ethical terms, would photos produced by all four processes be suitable for use in the family photo album?

Suppose the president's political party wants the photo for a reelection campaign's "Family Values" literature. Would photos produced by all four processes be equally ethical?

Would photos produced by all four processes be suitable for a daily newspaper's "day in the life of the president" story? A news magazine article about the man and his family? A general interest consumer magazine profile of the man and his family? Where do you draw the lines, and why?

One Possible Assessment

First, the credibility of images in a private album is a private matter. Doctoring family portraits might be interesting, even fascinating, but is it our business?

Would "photos" produced by all four processes be suitable for a daily newspaper? A news magazine? A general interest consumer magazine? All of these media have a responsibility to present realistic images (assuming none of them are overtly satirical). In the first two scenarios, if the photographer has to take many photos before finally capturing an acceptable image, the results might not be sterling examples of honesty, but they are not patently unethical, at least in terms of our discussion. Readers know that all of us, especially politicians, select flattering photos of ourselves. (The extent to which photo *selection* compromises objectivity is a worthy topic, but one outside our focus on photo manipulation.)

The third scenario is unacceptable because the digitization violates the viewfinder and process tests. Likewise in the fourth scenario, the composite is unacceptable for the same reasons.

Finally, regarding the reelection campaign's "Family Values" literature, the opinions expressed above apply: campaign literature may not be news, or journalism of any kind, but it carries at least a minimal implication of veracity.

Do you agree with this assessment? Why or why not?

SUMMARY

The tests can work side by side or overlap. For example, regarding the Diet Coke can (Figure 10.1), either nonfiction photography's process test or the viewfinder test could call into question the wisdom of running the photo without disclosure. Similarly, in the Harding/Kerrigan "photo" in *Newsday* (Chapters 4, 16) or the Tori Spelling photo in *Details* (Figure 17.1), the process and viewfinder tests again work hand in hand: Although the *Newsday* image was a composite and the *Details* image was a substantially manipulated photo, in both cases alterations that went beyond accepted processing techniques materially changed the image from what the photographer saw in the viewfinder.

Whether we apply one test or the other is secondary. Either way, the conclusion is the same: The photo lacks authenticity. Neither the technical credibility test nor the obvious implausibility test apply in any of these cases.

EXPLORATIONS

1. Review the altered photos listed in Chapter 4 under the heading "Other Examples in News, Sports, Entertainment, and More." Assume that all of them appear to be technically credible, i.e., realistic-looking. For each image, ask these questions:
   - What is the context of the photo? Consider the nature of the publication, the type of text and graphic elements you might expect to have appeared with the photo, and other aspects discussed in Chapter 9.
   - Given the photo's context, what is its implication of authenticity?

2. Consider a few of the published images reproduced in this book. For each one, ask these questions:
   - Did it appear in a nonfiction photographic environment?
   - Did the photo pass the viewfinder test?
   - Was it photofictional?
   - If so, was its fictional content obvious?
   - Was its fictional content the essence of the image?
   - If the photo was fictionalized, should it have been labeled?
   - How conspicuous should the label have been (discuss the label's location, size, and graphic treatment)?
   - Would the label have been sufficient to keep the photo from misleading readers?
   - Having considered all these elements, was the photo ethical as published? Would it have been ethical if labeled?

ENDNOTES

1. David Schonauer, "In Camera" column, *American Photo* (September/October 1998): 13.
2. From an e-mail correspondence with the author, fall 1998.
3. From an e-mail correspondence with the author, fall 1998.
4. Dan Gilgoff, "Gone but Never Forgotten," *U.S. News & World Report* (July 9–16, 2001): 44.

Chapter 19

Journalistic Photography Online

A Possible Future

For the first time in the history of commerce [the World Wide Web] has the potential to be a truly global market. It is also a medium in which photography shines. . . . The WWW offers to photographers the possibility of selling their work directly to the consumer for the first time. Imagine the possibilities. . . . This medium has the potential to save photojournalism.

—Peter Howe, Director of Photography and Sourcing, Corbis[1]

SILVER LINING: A NEW VISUAL JOURNALISM?

While many commentators warn that visual journalism's future is clouded by the digital environment and the World Wide Web, others seek a silver lining. *Time* magazine White House photographer Dirck Halstead predicted that the arrival of Web TV, an increase in the digital space available for content, and speedier digital delivery all will foster a need for a new kind of visual communicator, a "multitasker" who will work both in still and video technologies:

> New online publications, such as *The Digital Journalist*, will provide venues for visual storytellers . . . [Learning new techniques] takes time and a lot of hard work, but once mastered, along with an instinctive eye and the hunger to tell a story, a new kind of visual journalist and storyteller will emerge.[2]

Certainly, a whole new world of resources is already unfolding. Corbis, for example, is a privately owned company that provides images and services to professionals and consumers through digital technologies. The Corbis Collection houses some 25 million images of art and photography; more than 1.4 million are available online.

OUT WITH THE OLD?

If the future does indeed foster visual journalists of a new breed, will they use technology merely to disseminate the kinds of conventional photographs seen for decades in newspapers and the photorealistic fantasies seen for

> Is there hope for nonfiction photography? Of course. Nonfiction writing as a craft and calling wasn't demolished by the disintegration of The New Yorker and the rise of celebrity culture; it just sought new venues. And the effective death of Life magazine didn't kill photojournalism — it just sent it elsewhere. If anything, the easy access to increasingly inexpensive equipment and the ability to self-publish digitally should allow for a new flourishing of the craft. I believe that viewers' filters are quite sensitive, and after a period of adjustment they learn to distinguish the real from the unreal. After all, "staged photography" of one sort or another — fashion photographs, for example — has been for decades a staple in the same magazines that run photojournalism.
>
> — Randall Rothenberg[3]

years in magazines? Or might the processes of photography and the attitudes of its practitioners be reconfigured from the ground up, so as to cultivate something altogether new, an even more compelling and meaningful "eyewitness to history"? If traditional photojournalism dies or is relegated to obscurity, might something better take its place?

New York University Professor Fred Ritchin is the former picture editor of *The New York Times Magazine* and author of *In Our Own Image: The Coming Revolution in Photography* [Aperture, 1990; reissued, 1999]. In his 1998 article "Witnessing and the Web: An Argument for a New Photojournalism,"[4] he asserts that traditional photojournalism has partially failed for a variety of causes:

- a glut of set-up photos that merely re-create preconceived "looks"
- a preference for shocking images over serious ones ("most serious photography would be considered visually too low-key for today's press")
- superficiality, a preference for end results without explanations or context ("as if life is depicted by the tips of icebergs, the bottoms safely and knowingly left out of the way")
- stereotypes and generic imagery
- commercial pandering intended to seduce consumers rather than to inform readers;
- a voyeurism that reduces readers to anxiety and passivity, "unable to intercede with the grievous situations shown, unable even to understand why they exist"
- photography's false objectivity
- the photographer's role as a "bit player" who leaves the selection, captioning, design, and contextualization of photographs to others

- the limitations of fixed mechanical reproduction compared to fluid, real-time television and its "simultaneously connected audience"
- digital manipulation's intensification of existing public skepticism
- a lack of innovation among mainstream photojournalists in recent decades

IN WITH THE NEW?

But after detailing photojournalism's myths and shortcomings, Ritchin also envisions its revival in a radical, nonlinear and more meaningful form, involving:

> a simultaneous elevation of the photographer to author and his or her downgrading from authority to discussant; an overt embrace of certain aspects of media malleability, including its potentials for synergy; an active solicitation of divergent points of view as well as layers of context; and the empowerment of the reader and, whenever possible, the subject.[5]

In the very fluidity of the digital environment that has caused so many observers to fear for photojournalism's survival, Ritchin recognizes the potential for its resurrection. As he sees it, the digital domain allows the photograph to evolve from a fixed, two-dimensional image into a nonfixed, online "meta-photograph" (or whatever it comes to be called) that could function as a "node in a nonlinear, hypertextual environment"—a gateway to extended captions, other photos, audio, video, continually updated research resources, and so on, all of which could provide a richness of context impossible with fixed photography and text. Of course, readers would be informed that the online image is an example of this new "linking" strategy rather than a reproduction of a conventional photo.

With a click of the mouse, the viewer could perform the following tasks:

- access text information about people and scenes pictured in the photo far beyond the sorts of facts conveyed in typical captions
- view the "rejected" images also recorded at the scene, some of which may tell a different story or carry different implications than the "published" image
- see the lights, backdrop, and other equipment used to make the image, which would broaden viewers' appreciation of the manner in which it reflects reality
- view aspects of the scene outside the borders of the gateway image, which may also suggest different interpretations of reality
- read a bio of the photographer or access his or her Web site
- read text written about (or by) people pictured in the image

The viewer could register comments with the photographer and perhaps with the subject, or engage in a chat group with other concerned viewers. If

> Photographers need to respond to the computer the way painters responded to photography: Everything the painter held dear, the representation of reality, no longer held true, and so they went to Impressionism, Cubism. Photographers need to do that, to stop being scared about the future and just accept it.
>
> —Stephen Kroninger[6]

moved to do so, he or she could also access information about joining political groups, making contributions to causes, or other activities.

Certainly the Internet has begun to revolutionize the storage of, dissemination of, and access to photographs. In 2001, for example, Corbis announced that it would build an underground digitization facility for its collection of 17 million images.

SUMMARY

If this nonlinear web evolves into a major communications tool, viewers would negotiate it by a series of choices. No longer passive scanners and page-flippers, they would become involved with visual media to an unprecedented extent as active participants, eager to explore multiple meanings and layers of context scarcely hinted at in conventional photojournalism. Professor Ritchin states, "Photojournalism, in its new form, would be a much more profound strategy for witnessing the changing world in meaningful ways. . . . Ironically it may not be the linear photo essay that is eventually revived after its long decline, but a new essay form that makes the collage of television seem rather predictable."[7]

Other critics believe that this vision for the future of photography on the Internet is overly optimistic. At the very least, many questions remain. Who will own the images, and how will the images be captured, altered, edited, and presented? Who will control access, and how might their conscious or subconscious agendas or biases affect how the images are perceived by the public? Certainly, the same temptations of commerce—in regard to selling media as well as media advertisers' products—will continue to exert their influence.

EXPLORATIONS

1. Compare your own experiences of consuming nonfiction information in print and digital media. Start at the beginning—where you sit, your posture, the reading environment, how the words and images look on the page or screen. How do you move about among different images or sections of text? Compare page-turning to scrolling down

> I think a new language is being developed, just like photography was once a new language . . . now people can tell the difference between a painting and a photograph. Eventually, whether it's 50 years down the road or whatever, we'll have the same collective awareness about computers that people used to have about photography.
>
> —Matt Mahurin[8]

an online document. Consider the supplementary resources available in a typical textbook (footnotes, an index, table of contents, a bibliography) to the linked resources available on the Web.

What is the effect of all these differences on the way you perceive images? Do the physical properties of a textbook or an album of photos tend to guide you through the material in a certain way, as compared to your experiences online? What other differences in the way you perceive mass media can be traced to differences in the structure, organization and presentation of information in the print and digital realms?

2. When you pick up a book or a magazine, what aspects of context provide clues or cues as to its trustworthiness? Does your sense of its trustworthiness tend to change as you read it or flip through it? How does that compare to the online experience? For example, as you click through a dozen different links, must you reassess the trustworthiness of the material at various stops along the way?

3. Have you ever wondered if a particular online image or piece of text is fiction or nonfiction? What clues or cues are available to distinguish one from the other?

4. At the barber shop or salon you pick up a magazine whose cover catches your eye. Perhaps it's a *People*, with its story on whether female TV celebrities are too thin; a *National Geographic* revealing secrets of Mediterranean shipwrecks; or a *Consumer Reports* detailing the best values in home stereo systems. You scan it for fifteen minutes during your haircut. In terms of the information you're processing, what is the role of magazine staff members such as the photo editor or editor in chief? What corollaries exist, if any, when consuming mass media on the Internet?

ENDNOTES

1. Peter Howe, "Saving Photojournalism," *The Digital Journalist*, http://digitaljournalist.org/issue9809/howe.htm.
2. Dirck Halstead, "Looking Ahead to Photojournalism 2001," *The Digital Journalist*, http://digitaljournalist.org/issue9809/editorial.htm.

3. Randall Rothenberg has held senior editorial positions at *Wired, Esquire* and *The New York Times Sunday Magazine.* He is the author of several books, an award-winning feature writer and a contributor to *The Atlantic Monthly, The Nation* and many other magazines. In 1992 and 1993 he was a fellow at the Freedom Forum Media Studies Center at Columbia University. From an e-mail correspondence with the author, fall 1998.

4. Fred Ritchin, "Witnessing and the Web: An Argument for a New Photojournalism," XPoseptember catalog (Stockholm, 1998, edited by Carl Heideken): 167–93.

5. Ritchin, 175–76.

6. Stephen Kroninger is a photocollage illustrator and animator. Janet Abrams, "Little Photoshop of Horrors: The Ethics of Manipulating Journalistic Imagery," *Print* (November/December 1995): 28.

7. Ritchin, 167, 191.

8. Matt Mahurin is a digital photo artist. Abrams, 28.

Chapter 20

A Fragile Fortress of Credibility

New technologies don't come with instruction books of ethics. The ethics have to come from the minds and hearts of the creators and the editors of photographs and publications. Those publications wishing to be believed by readers must draw the line and take whatever steps are required to say, "What you see here, you can believe." A publication's integrity remains its most valued asset, and its most fragile.
—Bill Allen, *National Geographic*[1]

DEEPER MEANINGS

Where is the deeper meaning of a photograph to be found? The survival of photocredibility depends on public opinion, so for our purposes photographic meaning is to be found not in academic treatises, professional codes or textbooks; rather, it is found alongside the location of beauty—in the eye of the beholder. If a pre-exposure practice or post-exposure alteration changes what the viewer *thinks* a mass-media photo means, that is sufficient. Once informed of the practice or alteration, if viewers believe a purportedly journalistic image no longer qualifies as a "picture of reality," then the image is rendered potentially unethical. Whether its publication is ultimately unethical will depend on whether it is obviously implausible, appropriately labeled or otherwise qualified as discussed in earlier chapters.

In even nominally journalistic contexts, if our photofiction is not immediately obvious and the fiction is the essence of our image, or accounts for a substantial portion of its meaning—especially if consumers have to read fine print to discover it (perhaps only *after* buying our publication)—then we have tricked them. We have violated their qualified expectation of reality, their trust. Fine print or no fine print, we have lied to them, and we take the same risks all liars take.

> We expect our designers to refrain from any digital manipulation that might knowingly alter or combine image content in a way that could distort the original intent of the photographer. . . . We also do not condone the manipulation of news images in any manner that can alter the reader's perception of an event, place or person. The forms of digital manipulation we do support include simple cropping, silhouetting, vignetting, and shadow effects that are applied to enhance the page layout, and color enhancements and image cleaning that improve reproduction quality.
>
> — Richard Berenson, <u>Reader's Digest</u>[2]

A NEW VIGILANCE

In Chapter 10 we asked whether journalists in a media environment saturated in photofiction can maintain a fortress of credibility around authentic images, isolating them in the public mind from photo-illustrations and other contrivances. To do so requires first recognizing the possibility that public faith in photocredibility itself may diminish significantly in the near future. The apparent impartiality of photography's mechanical and chemical processes once helped foster popular allusions to phototruth: "photographic proof," "pictures don't lie," "seeing is believing" and so on. Photos seemed real. Exceptions were identified with any number of qualifiers: *trick, special-effects, doctored, manipulated.* All of these assumptions made policies regarding the ethics of altered photos seem uncomplicated, at least in comparison to the digital dilemmas we now face. But the liquid essence of digital technology may foster a new set of expressions, from now on acknowledging how fleeting, how impermanent, how unreal mass media images have become.

This shift from public faith to skepticism or outright distrust must be offset by a corresponding increase in professionals' commitments to honesty and clarity. However difficult it was to earn respect in the past, it will be more difficult in the future. We can no longer afford the comfort of asking the easy question: "Given public faith in photography, what must we do to avoid betraying it?" Instead, we face a tougher challenge: "Given well-founded skepticism of mass media in general and published imagery in particular, how can we demonstrate that at least some photos can still be believed?"

Any fortress of credibility visual journalists can construct will likely be a precarious one, a citadel in need of constant guarding, regular propping up, occasional repair. Publications that seek credibility will have to work hard to prove themselves. As readers of print and online media separate the

> I'm not all that pessimistic. . . . There are plenty of committed photojournalists still working, struggling to remain honorable to their work and their craft, and believing in the power of photographs that speak to certain truths and remain free of manipulation.
>
> — Bill Luster, President, NPPA[3]

trustworthy publications from all the others, writer and editor Randall Rothenberg's opinion that "credibility derives from the organization and its personnel, not from the medium" will become ever more acutely relevant.

A PROACTIVE APPROACH

Visual journalists committed to maintaining the public trust might consider any or all of the following strategies:

- Develop unambiguous protocols tailored to their own publications to ensure that nonfiction photos meet their implications of authenticity. Images that fall short should be rejected or appropriately labeled. At every step, err on the side of straightforward disclosure.
- Protocols and their supporting philosophies should be shared with the public—often—in publisher's columns, editor's notes, responses to readers' letters, masthead blurbs, and so on.
- Readers should be regularly invited to share in the process by attending publication-sponsored forums, contributing letters or guest columns, and so on.

TAKING THE PLEDGE

Many publications have already established protocols, but do readers know about them? Perhaps the American Society of Magazine Editors, the American Society of Newspaper Publishers, the National Press Photographers Association, the Society of Professional Journalists, and similar organizations could convene a joint committee to write a Pledge of Truth and Accuracy in Media Photography. Newspapers and magazines that sign on would be given permission to display a badge or symbol certifying their commitment. Readers should be informed of the process at the outset and regularly reminded of what the certification guarantees. Ideally, they then would be better able to distinguish publications committed to truthful photography. A joint public relations effort could bring the program to the attention of the public, professionals, commentators, and educators.

One News Group's Policy

Asserting that "there is no such thing as an 'innocent' alteration of a news photo," and that "the purpose of all editorial photography is to convey the scene as accurately as possible," the San Gabriel Valley Newspapers (Thomson L.A. News Group) policy states in part: "There will be no alteration of any photo, by any means, digital or conventional, for any purpose other than to enhance accuracy or to improve technical quality. If there is an element of a photo that is deemed unsuitable for publication, then that element may be cropped out or another frame chosen. Cloning and similar digital or conventional techniques are specifically forbidden to be used for this purpose. If the offending element may not be cropped out and there is no other suitable frame available, then no photo will run."[4]

Sample Pledge

The wording of the pledge should be jargon-free and directed to readers as well as media professionals. The following is a sample draft:

Our Pledge of Truth in Media Photography

In our publication, you can believe what you see. If we pose or "set up" a photo, you will know it because of the content of the photo itself, as when a person poses for a portrait, a fashion model displays items of clothing, children in a class picture stand in rows and all look at the camera, or objects are arranged to illustrate an article on camping gear, food preparation, and the like; any ambiguity will be cleared up in the caption or credit line. Otherwise, we don't set up photos. If it looks like a photo of an event or a moment that our photographer captured, then that's exactly what it is.

Once a photo has been taken, it is processed in accordance with long-established photojournalistic rules that guarantee that what you see is what the photographer saw through the viewfinder. We do allow traditional techniques such as trimming ("cropping") that does not mislead, cleaning negatives (or their digital equivalents), correcting color, improving contrast and the like. We do not add, delete, reposition or rearrange any people or objects, even tiny details, within the frame of a photo.

If we make exceptions to the policy detailed above, we will tell you what we did, and why. Legitimate examples might include a photo of a public school altered to illustrate how it would look if voters approved a renovation, or a satellite photo shaded to reveal a weather pattern. Disclosure of any such alteration will be spelled out in the caption itself so that it will not be missed.

Throughout their histories, newspapers and magazines have employed artists to illustrate some articles with cartoons, drawings, paintings, collages, and so on. With digital technology, entirely fictional or partially fictional illustrations can be made to look like photographs. We will avoid this technique unless we are sure readers will immediately recognize the image as fictional (as when a contemporary person's face appears on Mount Rushmore, for example), or the image is accompanied by a prominent, unambiguous label such as "computerized photofiction."

We intend for this policy to assist us in our efforts to use new technologies to do a better job of what ethical news publications have always done: inform, educate, and enlighten their readers. This is our pledge of integrity in visual journalism. We invite your comments.

Beyond Hard News

Modified versions of the pledge could be adopted by other nonfiction media such as online journals or general-interest consumer publications. A travel magazine might explain which sorts of photo alterations are acceptable and which are not. A car publication might specify that altered photos will be used only when prominently identified, as in this caption from the October 2001 *Road & Track*: "This computer-enhanced photo of Opel's 2003 Astra shows the radical shape that the 2004 Chevrolet Cavalier will take on." A woman's magazine that wanted to distance itself from the pack could let readers know that when processing photographs, altering body proportions is off-limits.

PHOTOGRAPHS STILL MATTER

Not so long ago it seemed that certain kinds of images could be counted upon to appear in certain places. While the compartmentalization was never airtight, one could expect generally consistent groupings of images within the fairly defined borders of newspapers, lifestyle magazines, "coffee table" nature books, supermarket tabloids and so on. But in a postmodern era of high tech, mixed media, and convergence, it almost seems as if all types of images are viewed everywhere all the time, blended as if by a Cuisinart. Some are glimpsed repeatedly but in wildly different contexts—deconstructed, reconstructed, reincarnated, semidisguised, dressed up, dressed down, Frankensteined, and cartoonified. By the late 1990s, when a wise-cracking TV chihuahua appeared under moody red skies in some sort of vaguely *communista* setting to sell fast-food tacos, it seemed conventional categories of iconography had indeed been laid to rest.

And yet even amid the visual confetti of contemporary media, photographs can still be real. Responsible magazines prove it every month, every week. Newspapers prove it every day. Photos continue to enlighten, inspire, bring a smile. They can still appall, pluck heartstrings, even change lives. A photo can still mean, I was there, this is a part of what I saw, and if you had been there you would have seen it too. This uniquely photographic quality of the frozen moment is precious, and worth saving.

> Will "unretouched" photos still be used in the future? Will readers appreciate them? Will photojournalism get at essential truth and try to plainly reveal ourselves as it has in the past? The answers are yes, yes, and yes. Certain media will be respected for their proximity to reality, just as they are today. Readers will know that some news organizations are more rigorous than others, more reliable.
> — Phil Hood, Alliance for Converging Technologies[5]

AUTHENTICITY MIGHT MAKE A STAND

After lamenting the Age of Falsification—"the fascination with virtual reality in a world teeming with real realities"—Kenneth Brower asserted: "Nature, in contrast, is always true. Throughout most of its history photography has been a chronicle of real moments. . . . Nature photography is one part of our culture where authenticity might make a stand."[6]

Will nonfiction photographers of all stripes and their editors and publishers make a stand for authenticity? Maintaining credibility will require a clarity of purpose, the courage and discipline to resist the almost irresistible temptation of undetectable tampering, a public information campaign conducted with enthusiasm on several fronts, and a continuing commitment to a standard articulated more than a decade ago by John Long:

> Each day when you step out onto the street, remember that you have been granted a sacred trust to be truthful. You have the responsibility to produce only honest images. You have no right to set up pictures; you have no right to stage the news; you have no right to distort the facts. Your fellow citizens trust you.[7]

Kenneth Brower once confessed to a slight disappointment after learning that one of his favorite Galen Rowell photos resulted from the photographer having asked the subject to repeat an action Rowell had witnessed. But Brower also made this observation: "The hard work of making a photograph is not like the easy work of looking at one, and a little crevasse will probably always lie between maker and viewer. Photography's task in the digital age will be to ensure that the crevasse does not erode into a chasm."[8]

Do our actions further erode that crevasse? Do our journalistic images mean what they seem to say? We must continue to ask these questions. The point is not whether such images are subject to the biases of the photographer or photo editor. Of course they are, like all published photos. The point is whether they have been set up or manipulated in such a way as to mislead viewers, to violate their Qualified Expectations of Reality.

> I know the earth is round by relying on the words of someone who has seen it and proved it with photographs. . . . You have to rely on a person who has already had this kind of experience and has no reason to tell lies.[9]
> — His Holiness the Dalai Lama, explaining the Buddhist concept of Extremely Hidden Phenomena

As presented here, this QER and its associated guidelines and tests are broadly cast to apply to all nonfiction mass-media photography. Of course, such photography encompasses different levels of implied authenticity and many types of publishing endeavors, with ethical standards of varying rigor. For example, editors at a daily newspaper may decide that a fictionalized photo would never accompany a "hard news" story, regardless of the image's implausibility or labeling.

In any case, the promise of a legitimate nonfiction photo is that it fulfills its implied authenticity; it means what it says. The survival of nonfiction visual media's credibility depends on whether we make good on that promise. In that regard, not much has changed. The ultimate test, as before, is a two-faceted standard of perception as well as honesty: Do our readers think we are truthful? Are they right?

ENDNOTES

1. From an e-mail correspondence with the author, fall 1998.
2. Richard Berenson is the worldwide art director of *Reader's Digest*. Excerpted from a fax sent to the author, August 10, 1994.
3. Bill Luster, "Photojournalism's Sorrows and Joys," *News Photographer* (October 1993): 11.
4. For another example, from *The Minnesota Daily*, see "The Minnesota Daily, Ethics Form," *News Photographer* (February 1995): 25.
5. Phil Hood is a senior analyst with the Alliance for Converging Technologies, Toronto, Ontario. From an e-mail correspondence with the author, fall 1998.
6. Kenneth Brower, "Photography in the Age of Falsification," *Atlantic Monthly* (May 1998): 108.
7. Quoted in Paul Lester, *Photojournalism: An Ethical Approach* (Hillsdale, NJ: Lawrence Erlbaum Associates, 1991), 132.
8. Brower, 109.
9. Brower, 106.

Photo Credits

Chapter 1. Page 7: Figure 1.1 by Louis Daguerre, © CORBIS/Bettmann. Page 8: Figure 1.2 © CORBIS. Page 10: Figure 1.3 courtesy George Eastman House. **Chapter 2.** Page 16: Figure 2.1 © Board of Trustees, National Gallery of Art; Figure 2.2 courtesy George Eastman House. Pages 20–21: Figure 2.5 courtesy David King Collection. **Chapter 3.** Page 29: Figure 3.1 © Art Wolfe/Tony Stone Images. Page 35: Figure 3.2 Star Wars: Episode I—The Phantom Menace © 1999 Lucasfilm Ltd. & TM. All rights reserved. Used under authorization. Courtesy of Lucasfilm Ltd. Pages 36–37: Figure 3.3 courtesy AP/Wide World Photos, Angela Perkins, c/o MIT. **Chapter 4.** Page 43: Figure 4.1 © Mary Ellen Mark. Page 46: Figure 4.2 courtesy Newsweek. Page 47: Figure 4.3 © 1997 Time Inc. Reprinted by permission. Page 49: Figure 4.4 courtesy Newsweek. Page 50: Figure 4.5 © Douglas Kirkland—Sygma. **Chapter 5.** Page 57: Figure 5.1 reprinted with permission of American Photo/Hachette Filipacchi Medias USA. Page 60: Figure 5.2 © 2001 Frans Lanting. Reprinted with permission. Page 62: Figure 5.3 © (Chris Crumley)/Earth Water Stock. Page 63: Figure 5.4 courtesy Mike Meadows/ Los Angeles Times Syndicate. **Chapter 7.** Page 83: Figure 7.1 courtesy George Eastman House. Page 86: Figure 7.3 courtesy Bill Eppridge/TimePix. Contributor(s): Eppridge, William. Page 87: Figure 7.4 courtesy Liaison Agency, Inc. **Chapter 8.** Page 95: Figure 8.1 courtesy Ben Trefny. **Chapter 9.** Page 106: Figure 9.1 © Los Angeles Police Department, courtesy Newsweek. **Chapter 10.** Pages 114–115: Figure 10.1 by J.B. Forbes/*St. Louis Post-Dispatch*. Page 123: Figure 10.2 photo by George Holtz from *Men's Journal*, March 1996, by Men's Journal Company. L.P. 1996. All rights reserved. Reprinted by permission. Page 124: Figure 10.3 © 1994 Time Inc. Reprinted by permission. **Chapter 14.** Page 150: Figure 14.1 reprinted with permission from the October 1990 issue of *Texas Monthly*. Page 151: Figure 14.2 © 1994 Gerald Bybee. Page 152: Figure 14.3 Gates by Ruben Sprich/Reuters/Timpix; "The Main Event" by Joe Zeff and Ed Gabel from *Time*, 6/1/98; Copyright © 1998 Time Inc. Reprinted by permission. Page 153: Figure 14.4 © 1992. Bobby Neel Adams/TimePix. Contributor(s): Adams Bobby Neel. Page 154: Figure 14.5 © 1991. Reprinted by permission of Psychology Today. Page 155: Figure 14.6 Lincoln and Monroe images © Bettmann/ CORBIS; digital image © Jack Harris/Visual Logic. Pages 156–157: Figure 14.7 © Troy House, 1996. Page 158: Figure 14.8 © 1993. Reprinted by permission of Psychology Today. Page 159: Figure 14.9 © Raul Vega Photo. Used with permission. *Esquire* is a trademark of Hearst Magazines Property, Inc. All rights reserved. **Chapter 15.** Page 164: Figure 15.1 © 1996 Time Inc. Reprinted by permission. **Chapter 16.** Page 172: Figure 16.1 by Deborah Feingold, 1985, by Straight Arrow Publishers, Inc. All rights reserved. Reprinted by permission. Page 176: Figure 16.2 © Brenda Priddy and Company. **Chapter 17.** Page 184: Figure 17.1 reprinted with permission of American Photo, Hachette Filipacchi Medias USA.

Name Index

Subject Index